faith

The Link With God's Power

Publishers Since 1798

THOMAS NELSON PUBLISHERS
Nashville

Reinhard Bonnke

Published in Nashville, Tennessee, by Thomas Nelson, Inc.

Unless otherwise noted Scripture quotations are from THE NEW KING JAMES VERSION. Copyright © 1979, 1980, 1982, Thomas Nelson, Inc., Publishers.

Scripture quotations noted NIV are from the HOLY BIBLE: NEW INTER-NATIONAL VERSION®. Copyright © 1973, 1978, 1984 by International Bible Society. Used by permission of Zondervan Publishing House. All rights reserved.

Scripture quotations noted KJV are from the KING JAMES VERSION of the Holy Bible.

Library of Congress Cataloging-in-Publication Data

Bonnke, Reinhard.
    Faith: the link with God's power / Reinhard Bonnke.
        p. cm.
    ISBN 0-7852-7469-3
    1. Faith—Biblical teaching. I. Title.
BS680.F27.B66 1998

                            98-20603
                              CIP

Printed in the United States of America
1 2 3 4 5 6 7 DHC 04 03 02 01 00 99 98

Contents

Foreword

This book comes to you with a fresh angle on the subject of faith. It offers profound insights into its trials and triumphs, and puts the spotlight on God's character and His Word. Here is just one brief example of how Scripture illustrates the relationship between faith and feelings.

When danger looms large, fear is inevitable. When our body chemistry sets up a sense of impending disaster, when we suffer heavy blows and our circumstances are oppressive and dark, or when pain and illness sit with us at the fireside, fear and alarm are a natural response. What, then, does faith do? It takes the shackles from our ankles; we challenge the paralyzing grip and go ahead anyway. With God, fear will not stop us—we overcome it. "Why are you cast down, O my soul? / And why are you disquieted within me? / Hope in God, for I shall yet praise Him / For the help of His countenance" (Ps. 42:5).

Blessings unfold with each chapter, the focus being firmly set on Jesus Christ, "the author and finisher of our faith" (Heb. 12:2).

My desire is, through this book, to teach the never-changing faith principles revealed in the Word of God. They have been proven in my own fifty years of following Jesus against the backdrop of decades of front-line evangelism across the world. The same principles have been tried and tested by my colleague, the Reverend George Canty from the United Kingdom. His scholarly collaboration with me as I prepared the manuscript is something for which I am deeply grateful.

Reinhard Bonnke
Frankfurt, Germany, March 1998

Faith: The Sixth Sense?

There are some extraordinary ideas about faith floating around in the world—so bizarre in fact that we need to clarify what we are discussing. Some believe that just having faith entitles one to blessings and prosperity. Others believe that faith in oneself is all that's needed in life. And still others feel that faith, in and of itself, is a cosmic force that breeds superhuman, superspiritual, invincible people.

It is none of that. Having faith does not mean believing what you know isn't true or believing something for which there is no evidence. The Bible is a big book all about faith and all about the evidence that makes faith so vital, so important, and so astounding.

According to the book of Hebrews, "faith is the substance of things hoped for, the evidence [or realization/confidence] of things not seen" (11:1), and yet the Bible explains faith in detail, unlike anything we have ever read.

"By faith," the Bible says, "we understand that the worlds were framed by the word of God, so that the things which are

Through Faith God's people can accomplish "the miraculous"

> Having faith does not mean believing what you know isn't true or believing something for which there is no evidence.

seen were not made of things which are visible" (Heb. 11:3). Far more than a mere statement, though, this faith Scripture is corroborated by a list of examples in the same book:

"By faith Abel offered to God a more excellent sacrifice than Cain, through which he obtained witness that he was righteous, God testifying of his gifts; and through it he being dead still speaks" (v. 4).

And, "By faith Enoch was taken away so that he did not see death, 'and was not found, because God had taken him'; for before he was taken he had this testimony, that he pleased God" (v. 5).

And verse 6 tells why Enoch pleased God. "But without faith it is impossible to please Him, for he who comes to God must believe that He is, and that He is a rewarder of those who diligently seek Him." Throughout Hebrews chapter 11, the evidence is overwhelming, stating over and over that, through faith, people accomplished the miraculous.

Faith's Roll of Honor

Noah, who moved with godly fear in preparing the ark; Abraham, who was called by God to go to a place he had no knowledge of, and further offered his own son, Isaac, as a sacrifice to God, knowing that God would protect Isaac; Sarah, who conceived *after* she was unable to do so; Joseph, who made mention of the children of Israel departing from Egypt and gave instructions concerning his bones; and Moses, who refused to be called the son of Pharaoh's daughter, choosing rather to suffer affliction with the people of God than to enjoy the passing pleasures of sin, esteeming the reproach of Christ as greater riches than the treasure of Egypt.

You see, by faith, Moses forsook Egypt, not fearing the wrath of the king; for he endured as seeing Him who is invisible. By faith he kept the Passover and the sprinkling of blood, lest he who destroyed the firstborn should touch them. And "by faith they passed through the Red Sea as by dry land, whereas the Egyptians, attempting to do so, were drowned" (vv. 27–29).

Hebrews 11 is considered a roll of honor, listing heroes and heroines of faith, these people are remembered not for valor or kindness, but for their complete reliance upon God.

Faith is a perfectly ordinary thing that makes us outstanding in the eyes of God. By faith it is possible to please God, and faith is possible to everybody. *AMEN! → Glory God!*

The elementary fact is that faith is power through God, His Word, and His faithfulness. Faith is "built-in." By that I mean we are born believers. If you think you have no faith, try *not* believing in anything or anybody—your wife, husband, doctor, bank, boss, baker, or chef. We put our lives into the

> **Faith is possible to everybody.**

hands of surgeons and trust train engineers, cabbies, and pilots without thinking of faith, but that's exactly what it is.

Faith—A Part of Life

Stop using this faculty of faith and you would never get out of bed in the morning or step outside. You would fancy the sky might fall down. In this world a million cobra troubles are coiled to strike, but we carry on, usually quite regardless and confident. The Bible says, "God hath dealt to every man the measure of faith" (Rom. 12:3b KJV). Christ said, "Only believe" (Mark 5:36), because we can.

Faith is a kind of immune system filtering out fears that otherwise would paralyze all activity. When it fails we develop all kinds of phobias and compulsions. Jesus said not to have phobia, but faith.

[handwritten annotations: FeAr / FAith is GOD's belief/belief in GOD's power, / Fear is the Devil's Faith To DeThrone GOD's power,]

Putting Faith to Work

During the years of our tent crusades in Africa, my music minister, Adam Mtsweni, and I were looking for a new platform organ and went from shop to shop in the city of Johannesburg. It was noon, and there was one more shop to visit. On arrival I saw a salesman hanging around during the lunch break, and I thought he had hardly noticed us. My colleague and I went from instrument to instrument, but suddenly that lone salesman stood in front of me. His eyes were wide open and his face was as white as a sheet. "Sir," he stammered, "I can see Jesus in your eyes." I was dumbfounded. *How can this be?* I thought, *A total stranger says he can see Jesus in my eyes?* We had something like a revival in the music shop, and when I left, walking to the car, I said, "Lord, I will never understand how something like this is possible." Then the Holy Spirit spoke

> Faith is a kind of immune system filtering out fears that otherwise would paralyze all activity.

to me: "No problem! Through faith, Jesus lives in your heart, and sometimes He likes to look out of the windows!" What a wonderful truth. In John 14:23, Jesus said, "If anyone loves Me, he will keep My word; and My father will love him, and We will come to him and make Our home with him."

Furthermore, we read in Luke that while Jesus was speaking to a crowd, "someone came from the ruler of the synagogue's house, saying to him, 'Your daughter is dead. Do not trouble the Teacher.'"

> But when Jesus heard it, He answered him, saying, "Do not be afraid; only believe, and she will be made well." When He came into the house, He permitted no one to go in except Peter, James, and John, and the father and mother of the girl. Now all wept and mourned for her; but He said, "Do not weep; she is not dead, but sleeping." And they rediculed Him, knowing that she was dead.
>
> But He put them all outside, took her by the hand and called, saying, "Little girl, arise." Then her spirit returned, and she arose immediately. And He commanded that she be given something to eat. (8:49–55)

On the surface you might conclude that it takes a lot of faith to believe that Jesus could, or would, cure your daughter of an illness, let alone raise her from the dead. But it takes no more or no less faith in God to do that than to give us our daily supply of food or shelter. We serve a big God, and He is able to do whatever we ask of Him—not because we have faith enough, but because we have faith, period.

[handwritten: Faith Has no Feeling—It is Just There!]

[handwritten: Faith is Just FAITH!]

Being the Good Father

Jesus told of God's goodness and willingness to help all of us. In Luke, chapter 11, He told a parable about the "good father":

> *[handwritten: MAT. 7:— GOOD GIFTS]*
> *[handwritten: LUKE 11: The Holy Spirit]*
> If a son asks for bread from any father among you, will he give him a stone? Or if he asks for a fish, will he give him a serpent instead of a fish? Or if he asks for an egg, will he offer him a scorpion? If you then, being evil, know how to give good gifts to your children, how much more will your heavenly Father give the Holy Spirit to those who ask Him! (vv. 11–13)

Nevertheless, people confuse faith with virtue. Faith is there. Faith is just faith. Virtue is developed. Faith doesn't come as does learning the piano grade by grade. People talk about "big believers," as if believing came in sizes like suit jackets. We can have faith even when we know we are not very good. Nonbelievers can have faith, otherwise they could never be brought to the realization that Jesus Christ is Lord.

All Can Believe

That very same Lord of lords taught us that all can believe in Him. He said so in John 14:1. But Scripture also says something extraordinary about faith. "He indeed was foreordained before the foundation of the world, but was manifest in these last times for you who through Him believe in God, who raised Him from the dead and gave Him glory, so that your faith and hope are in God" (1 Peter 1:20–21). Through Christ alone, nonbelievers can believe!

Faith: The Sixth Sense?

But believe in what? Some believe in UFOs, that "mother earth" is alive, or that the dead really communicate with us. Surveys show that practically everybody believes in some sort of God, somewhere.

Believing tests us. The kind of God we believe in is a window into our soul. We are what we believe and in what we have faith. By way of illustration, Jesus talks about His equality with God in John 5:23–24 and the difference between a person who believes in Him and one who doesn't. "He who does not honor the Son does not honor the Father who sent Him," Jesus explained. "Most assuredly, I say to you, he who hears My word and believes in Him who sent Me has everlasting life, and shall not come into judgment, but has passed from death into life."

> Belief in Jesus Christ as God gives us life without end in the full presence of God Himself.

In other words, he who believes in Christ begins a new spiritual life—a quality relationship with God. We obtain a fullness of spiritual vitality that we lacked before believing in and having faith in God. **Belief in Jesus Christ as God gives us life without end in the full presence of God Himself.** This in and of itself constitutes a tremendous incentive to vigorously spread the gospel to those who still do not know its power and compassion.

The Needed Response

Belief, though, is much more than just knowledge of Christ. There must be a response to that belief system. Do we do

Belief In God without expectation is
A → Contrary To The Bible! (Pilot & Plane
example!)

Faith

what we believe? If we believe in a seed, we plant it and patiently wait for it to grow. A man who owns a plane but won't risk flying it is contrary to the pilot's character. And believing in God without expectation that He will do something is contrary to the entire Bible's message.

James, the half brother of Jesus, made some hard-hitting remarks about believing and faith in his epistle to Jewish believers who were struggling in their own faith. He saw them as succumbing to impatience, bitterness, materialism, disunity, and spiritual apathy. As a resident of Jerusalem and an early church leader, James had frequent contact with Jewish Christians and felt a responsibility to exhort and encourage them in their struggles of faith. To strengthen the early believers, James taught them that faith proves itself by works: *good works!*

> Believing in God without expectation is contrary to the entire Bible's message.

What does it profit, my brethren, if someone says he has faith but does not have works? Can faith save him? If a brother or sister is naked and destitute of daily food, and one of you says to them, "Depart in peace, be warmed and filled," but you do not give them the things which are needed for the body, what does it profit? Thus also faith by itself, if it does not have works, is dead. (James 2:14–17) *2 : 17*

James gave us the blueprint of what faith is and what it does. Its characteristics are unmistakable. **Faith** obeys the word of God, removes discrimination from our hearts, proves itself by works, controls the tongue, generates wisdom, exalts humility, and overwhelmingly produces a deep dependence on God.

In conjunction, faith triumphs when we pray for the afflicted and even when we confront the errors of our brother. "Brethren," James wrote, "if anyone among you wanders from the truth, and someone turns him back, let him know that he who turns a sinner from the error of his way will save a soul from death and cover a multitude of sins" (5:19–20).

> **Faith overwhelmingly produces a deep dependence on God.**

How to View God

There is yet another aspect of faith that is vital to our destiny as children of the Most High God. Faith, you see, is the portal by which we view and perceive God. He is Spirit. Mortal eyes are too weak to discern "the invisible God," "the King eternal, immortal" (Col. 1:15; 1 Tim. 1:17). We have to seek Him where He is found. "He who comes to God must believe that He is, and that He is a rewarder of those who diligently seek Him" (Heb. 11:6).

Some fall short of the fullness of belief in God because they trust their own senses more than Scripture. Wanting a God they can see has led many people to serious spiritual errors in judgment and has called their very faith into account. Thomas, one of the twelve disciples, was just such a person.

After the resurrection of Jesus, the countryside was ablaze with an uneasy excitement. One night, when the disciples, except Thomas, were gathered together in one place, Jesus appeared to them, blessed them, breathed the Holy Spirit on them, and said, "If you forgive the sins of any, they are forgiven them; if you retain the sins of any, they are retained" (John 20:23).

But when Thomas returned, the other disciples told him what had happened. He didn't believe them. "Unless I see in His hands the print of the nails," he said, "and put my finger into the print of the nails, and put my hand into His side, I will not believe" (John 20:25). A scant eight days later, the disciples were again gathered, but this time

> Some fall short of the fullness of belief in God because they trust their own senses more than Scripture.

Thomas was with them. Jesus again appeared. He looked at Thomas and said, "Reach your finger here, and look at My hands; and reach your hand here, and put it into My side. Do not be unbelieving, but believing." *JN. 20:29!*

Thomas must have felt terrible as he cried out to Jesus, "My Lord and my God!" But Jesus, looking at Thomas, said, "Thomas, because you have seen Me, you have believed. Blessed are those who have not seen and yet have believed" (John 20:26–29).

Not seeing is no reason for not believing. Nobody sees radiation. We wait for its effects. Nobody sees God, but millions find the effects of Him in their lives. Things happen that can only be from Him. Even one prayer answered, one healing, one miracle, one deliverance from addiction is evidence of Him.

But it isn't just one. Millions are healed, millions are delivered, millions of prayers are answered, and millions

Faith is not what you Have!, But What you Do w/it!

have had experiences that can only be attributed to Jesus Christ, risen from the dead, *Alive, living & Responding to Petitions for your Will!*

When I step on a platform in Africa or India or anywhere else, past biblical miracles collide with God's present-day mercy and grace. Without any touch of mine the blind begin to see, the deaf hear, the dumb speak, the crippled walk, and those driven to madness by clinging spirits of evil are released. The greatest effect is deliverance from sin and guilt and the transformation of people's attitudes and personalities.

> **Not seeing is no reason for not believing.**

The Gospel of John, chapter 20, verses 30 and 31, says: "Truly Jesus did many other signs in the presence of His disciples, which are not written in this book; but these [signs] are written that you may believe that Jesus is the Christ, the Son of God, and that believing you may have life in His name."

In other words, believing is not beyond us. Some think of faith in the same way they view money—a good thing if you have some. But faith is not what you have; it is what you do *w/it!* Just as we can see, hear, feel, taste, or smell, we can believe and act on that belief. And that act of faith is our true spiritual strength. It is our sixth sense or faculty—spiritual eyesight, an ear to hear, a hand to take God's blessing, and the courage to hold on to God's healing touch. But faith is not something we acquire in abundance, immediately upon recognizing and committing our lives to God.

When we encounter Jesus Christ for the first time, we are like children who find out for themselves who He was and is. We go from little or no faith in Him as the Son of God to fully understanding who He was and is and why He came to us as a simple child born in a manger.

The incident of Christ healing the blind man in John 9 shows how our faith can go from little to great—sometimes in a remarkably short period of time: Jesus came upon a blind man, and told His disciples, "As long as I am in the world, I am the light of the world" (v. 5). He then spat on the ground and made clay with His saliva, and then anointed the eyes

> Faith is not what you have; it is what you do.

of the blind man with the clay and said to him, "Go, wash in the pool of Siloam" (v. 7). The blind man went and washed there and came back seeing. Later he learned that it was Jesus who had performed this miracle. When the man's neighbors asked how it could be that he could see he said, "A Man called Jesus made clay and anointed my eyes and said to me, 'Go to the pool of Siloam and wash.' So I went and washed, and I received sight" (v. 11). That is where it stood—Jesus, a man.

However, faith began to arise. First, some of the Pharisees asked, "How can a man who is a sinner do such signs?" There was a division among them, so they asked the man who was healed who Jesus was, and he said, "He is a prophet" (v. 17).

The Pharisees didn't believe that this man was blind from birth, so they sent for his parents. His parents said, "We know that this is our son, and that he was born blind; but by what means he now sees we do not know, or who opened his eyes we do not know. He is of age; ask him. He will speak for himself" (vv. 20–21). The leading Jews had agreed to excommunicate from the synagogue anybody who said that Jesus was the Christ; so faced with such a fact as a man born blind made to see again, they questioned the man further. "Give God the glory!" they said. "We know that this Man is a sinner" (v. 24).

Developing Faith

The man then said, "Whether He is a sinner or not I do not know. One thing I know: that though I was blind, now I see" (v. 25). Then the man, who was arguing with the Pharisees about his healing, said, "If this Man were not from God, He could do nothing" (v. 33). This man's faith was developing, and he believed Christ was not a sinner, but from God. For this he suffered persecution and was blamed as being a disciple of Jesus.

Jesus then found the man. The authorities had thrown him out of the temple—typical of a world that rejects those who testify to the goodness of God. He had one important question to ask the man. It wasn't whether he felt grateful or if he had started to work. He asked, "Do you believe in the Son of God?" The man did not know what Jesus meant and said, "Who is He, Lord, that I may believe in Him?" (vv. 35–36).

He had enough faith in Jesus to feel his way to the pool of Siloam when he was blind because Jesus told him to go. That brought him physical sight. But another kind of faith could bring him far greater illumination. His faith had not reached that point. Then Jesus said, "You have both seen Him and it is He who is talking with you." The man looked at Christ, and his faith exploded. He had no problem accepting Christ's declaration. He said, "Lord, I believe!" Then, "He worshiped him" (vv. 37–38). Faith was complete.

The account of the woman of Samaria in the Gospel of John, chapter 4, is another powerful lesson from the history of faith. It is an illustration of the fact that a sinner can take a profound leap of faith into the heights of the supernatural.

A nameless woman came to draw water from a well at the same time Jesus was resting there from a hot, long walk. He asked her for a drink of water, which astonished her. She thought He was an odd sort of Jew to be so free, breaking all Jewish tradition by speaking to a Samaritan.

> "How is it that You, being a Jew, ask a drink from me, a Samaritan woman?" For Jews have no dealings with Samaritans. Jesus answered and said to her, "If you knew the gift of God, and who it is who says to you, 'Give Me a drink,' you would have asked Him, and He would have given you living water." The woman said to Him, "Sir, You have nothing to draw with, and the well is deep. Where then do You get that living water? Are You greater than our father Jacob, who gave us the well, and drank from it himself, as well as his sons and his livestock?" Jesus answered and said to her, "Whoever drinks of this water will thirst again, but whoever drinks of the water that I shall give him will never thirst. But the water that I shall give him will become in him a fountain of water springing up into everlasting life." (vv. 9–14)

At that point she decided to humor Him, so she just said, "Sir, give me this water, that I may not thirst, nor come here to draw." She certainly expected nothing of the kind. Jesus simply said, "Go, call your husband, and come here." She put on an air of innocence and said she had no husband.

Jesus then shattered her with a recitation of her sullied life and her Hollywood-like record of husbands. The woman stared at Him, shocked, and said, "Sir, I perceive that You are a prophet." She had advanced in her perception and in her faith.

The woman then said something that represented four hundred years of argument about where to worship: "Our fathers worshiped on this mountain, and you Jews say that in Jerusalem is the place where one ought to worship." Jesus then shook her ideas about worship. Worship had nothing to do with place or time. Worship was anywhere, everywhere, and always.

> Woman, believe Me, the hour is coming when you will neither on this mountain, nor in Jerusalem, worship the Father. You worship what you do not know; we know what we worship, for salvation is of the Jews. But the hour is coming, and now is, when the true worshipers will worship the Father in spirit and truth; for the Father is seeking such to worship Him. God is Spirit, and those who worship Him must worship in spirit and truth. (vv. 21–24).

The people God wanted were those whose worship was not confined to a local spot or fixed schedule. She felt lost now in such theological depth, so she tried to edge around it. She said such matters would be settled when the Messiah came.

The woman was getting closer, and then Jesus said, "I who speak to you am He." Her faith again soared. She looked at this man who saw her past like a filmed record and swept her out of her depth with His profound teaching. Excited, she rushed into the town telling everybody about

Jesus. "Come, see a Man who told me all things that I ever did." She then asked of the town's people, "Could this be the Christ?" Many men then went back to the well to see who this man was that had so affected her. They, too, fell under His divine spell and invited Him to stay in the town. For two days He was among them, and many more believed because of His own word. Then they said to the woman, "Now we believe, not because of what you said, for we ourselves have heard Him and we know that this is indeed the Christ, the Savior of the world."

The Development of Faith

In each of these incidents, the development of faith is swift and always ends with commitment to a relationship with Jesus Christ. Becoming a believer in God may not be an easy transition, but it is a gap that can be leaped as fast as light. One minute we are far from God, and the next we are bound to Him eternally through faith. In an instant we become as His disciples had become—"They are Yours. . . . and Yours are Mine, and I am glorified in them. . . . and none of them is lost" (John 17:9–12).

A Different Kind of Faith

Faith in Christ is different from any other kind of faith. In the New Testament, the word used means to believe "into" Christ (Greek, *eis*). That word suggests movement. The ordinary word for "in" (Greek, *en*) describes a set position, but the Greek word used for faith *in* Christ means moving close to Him in trustful love. It is an embrace.

This kind of loving touch between man and his Maker comes only through Christ.

This kind of loving touch between man and his Maker comes only through Christ. No one in the Old Testament days could think of such a thing. God was Spirit, another kind of Being, holy and too awesome to be approached except with fear and trembling. Yet one inspired book in the Old Testament Scriptures touches the heart of a new experience—the Song of Solomon, a lyric of love that gathers up all its words of supreme love in one phrase, "I am my beloved's, / And my beloved is mine" (6:3).

The Great Beloved One

When Jesus came, the Song of Solomon was fulfilled. He is the great beloved One. The dry, loveless religious world of the Jews had no spiritual experience that corresponded to the Song of Solomon. Any passionate embrace between heaven and earth was unknown until Jesus came. He is the divine Lover, and we are those He came to love.

A woman emptied a flask of priceless ointment upon the feet of Christ in holy adoration (John 12:1–8); a street-girl washed His feet with the water of her eyes, toweled them with her hair, and anointed them with oil and in love (Luke 7:37–47); a hard-hearted tax collector went wild with joy and wanted to give his money away (Luke 19:1–10); and Jerusalem had never seen anything like that—this monumental kind of adoring wonder that had all but changed the hearts of an entire nation.

And why not? Jesus began it Himself, as we read in John 13:1–12. At the Last Supper, when Jesus knew that the hour had come that He should depart from this world to the Father, having loved His own who were in the world, He loved them to the end. Jesus rose from the supper and laid aside His garments, took a towel, and girded Himself.

The Coming Dawn

That was the Lord God whom everyone could fling his or her arms around. His mother, Mary, did and so did Mary Magdalene, the former prostitute who was saved by the loving touch of the Master (Matt. 27:56–61).

In the Old Testament, revelation came to people about God, but it seemed to be only to rare individuals, such as Abraham, Jacob, and the prophets. The masses moved very slowly—and often moved backward. God used various circumstances and methods to help them to have faith. But the coming of Jesus swept the world. Somehow, Calvary does what the awesome manifestations of Sinai couldn't do. Jesus is the great Creator of faith. Looking back over the long, cheerless world history of uncertainty and doubt, we can see when it changed. It came with the gospel. It awakened sleeping trust. The dawn had come.

chapter 2

Faith in Three Tenses

There is an old saying asserting that "today, yesterday knocks on our door telling us about tomorrow." In other words, **what we believe will happen tomorrow comes from what we already know has happened yesterday.**

But to believe that takes faith. Faith can snap us out of our snug, little burrows and get us going for God. For example, this book coincides with the world-sized job God gave me: to publish and distribute first-class gospel material to every home. I have no money for such a fantastic scheme, but I have faith, committing myself to millions of dollars.

However, it is not faith built on faulty hopes. It is the faith in God today based on what He has already done. You see, I saw God meet this very same need in the British Isles, Germany, Austria, Switzerland, Sweden, Denmark, and Hong Kong, so I have good

> What we believe will happen tomorrow comes from what we already know has happened yesterday.

reason to believe that the publication of this book will signify that we put the gospel into every dwelling in Canada and the United States.

No matter with whom we deal, we don't know what they will be like, but we just take it on faith that if they have been trustworthy in the past, they will also be now. We all know that circumstances change, and sometimes we just have to take a chance. There's no other way. **Faith is a fact of life, like the need to breathe.**

God's Proven Track Record

I trust God because He has a proven track record. He has always taken care of me in the past. Like the weather, life in general is a matter of succinct probabilities, save one very important thing: the will of God. God is not affected by change, and God's will is the key to bring order from chaos.

Placing Your Bets

During my years as a missionary-evangelist in South Africa I sometimes was invited to participate in panel discussions on national television. We were to "discuss religious questions." One day an intellectual atheist confronted me. He was a great debater and thought he knew it all. When the discussion began I was dismayed. The atheist and the moderator began to speak about horse-racing, a subject I knew nothing about. The atheist was in his element. He knew the names of many horses and jockeys by heart and said, "I have put my money on such-and-such horse." At that moment the Holy

Spirit quickened me, and I said, "Mister, now I would like to tell you something about horses. I have put all my money on the white horse in the book of Revelation!" The atheist was baffled and repeated to himself, "White horse in the book of Revelation?" It seems to have been the only horse this horse expert had never heard of. Then he said, "Tell me preacher, who is the rider of that horse?" It sounded to me as if he wanted to know the name of the jockey. He couldn't have asked a better question. "Revelation chapter 19 tells us that the name of the rider is Faithful and True, it is the Lord Jesus Christ, the King of kings and the Lord of lords," I replied. "I want to be honest with you," I continued. "I didn't put money on Him, because I have no money. But I put my life and soul on Him, and I know that I am going to win!" This is where the race begins for God's people, with the absolute certainty that we are on the winning side. In John 16:33, Jesus says, "Take heart! I have overcome the world" (NIV).

> Faith is a fact of life, like the need to breathe.

God's Personality

In the book of Hebrews, we catch a glimpse of God's personality, commitment, and love:

Let your conduct be without covetousness; be content with such things as you have. For He Himself has said, "I will never leave you nor forsake you." So we may boldly say: "The LORD is my helper; I will not fear. What can man do to me?" Remember those who rule over you, who have spoken the word of God to you, whose faith follow, considering the outcome of their conduct. Jesus Christ is the same yesterday, today, and forever. (13:5–8)

Present Tense Faith

From this we can deduce that there are three tenses of faith. First, the apostle Paul, in writing a kind of thank-you note to the believers at Philippi for their help in his hour of need, profoundly asserted that "being confident of this very thing, that He who has begun a good work in you will complete it until the day of Jesus Christ;

> The Christian confidence is that what God was, He is and will be.

just as it is right for me to think this of you all, because I have you in my heart, inasmuch as both in my chains and in the defense and confirmation of the gospel, you all are partakers with me of grace" (Phil. 1:6–7). **The Christian confidence is that what God was, He is and will be.** Next, the Psalms admonish us to trust in the Lord and not be afraid:

The LORD is my light and my salvation;
Whom shall I fear?
The LORD is the strength of my life;
Of whom shall I be afraid?
When the wicked came against me
To eat up my flesh,

My enemies and foes,
They stumbled and fell.
Though an army may encamp against me,
My heart shall not fear;
Though war may rise against me,
In this I will be confident. (27:1–3)

His will cannot be challenged or changed for it shapes the future. And finally, we find that in His will, not ours or the world's, we are forever secure.

Do not love the world or the things in the world. If anyone loves the world, the love of the Father is not in him. For all that is in the world—the lust of the flesh, the lust of the eyes, and the pride of life—is not of the Father but is of the world. And the world is passing away, and the lust of it; but he who does the will of God abides forever. (1 John 2:15–17)

In other words, the man who does the will of God lives forever. By His Holy Word

Past Tense Faith

Some believers, though, have a past tense faith—they have no problem believing that God has done mighty works throughout history. In fact, **some people can believe anything if it took place a long time ago or will take place a long time in the future.** They can accept a partial promise, such as "And we know that all things work together for good to those who love God, to those who are the called according to His purpose" (Rom. 8:28). But to believe that, we also must take into account that verse in context:

> Now He who searches the hearts knows what the mind of the Spirit is, because He makes intercession for the saints according to the will of God. And we know that all things work together for good to those who love God, to those who are the called according to His purpose. For whom He foreknew, He also predestined to be conformed to the image of His Son, that He might be the firstborn among many brethren. Moreover whom He predestined, these He also called; whom He called, these He also justified; and whom He justified, these He also glorified." (Rom. 8:27–30)

Additionally, past tense faith people have extreme difficulty with a present tense promise like the one in Exodus that proclaims, "If you diligently heed the voice of the LORD your God and do what is right in His sight, give ear to His commandments and keep all His statutes, I will put

> Some people can believe anything if it took place a long time ago or will take place a long time in the future.

none of the diseases on you which I have brought on the Egyptians. **For I am the LORD who heals you**" (15:26).

They have a past but not a present faith. They believe in the God of Moses and Elijah and that Jesus did work miracles and that the Holy Spirit empowered the disciples. But that is hollow believing unless it transfers to today, believing that God will carry on the good work.

Could a God of such creative imagination settle down to be a God of the past, merely sitting in heaven with His hands folded in his lap? Could He fill the empty skies with unsurpassable beauty and then go to sleep? Is that a rational theory? Could any of us build a house and then abandon it? Could God ignore His own universe?

> "For I am the LORD who heals you."

The first book of Genesis affirms God's commitment and omnipotence:

> In the beginning God created the heavens and the earth. The earth was without form, and void; and darkness was on the face of the deep. And the Spirit of God was hovering over the face of the waters. Then God said, "Let there be light"; and there was light. And God saw the light, that it was good; and God divided the light from the darkness. God called the light Day, and the darkness He called Night. So the evening and the morning were the first day. (vv. 1–5)

The question here is, Why? Why would God do this? He didn't do it to please anybody—there wasn't anybody around, only Himself! He pleased Himself when He did it. He was not obliged to do so. No compulsion rested upon Him. He was not pressured. He wanted to do it.

Furthermore, God also brought the glittering stars and the planets into being. Psalm 19 begins,

> The heavens declare the glory of God;
> And the firmament shows His handiwork.

Day unto day utters speech,
And night unto night reveals knowledge.
There is no speech nor language
Where their voice is not heard.
Their line has gone out through all the earth,
And their words to the end of the world.
In them He has set a tabernacle for the sun,
Which is like a bridegroom coming out of his chamber,
And rejoices like a strong man to run its race.
Its rising is from one end of heaven,
And its circuit to the other end;
And there is nothing hidden from its heat. (vv. 1–6)

David, the author of this psalm, was obviously elated while penning it. But it is the aura of God, not the splendor of the universe, he is excited about. He is distracted from creation by the Creator, and what a marvelous distraction it is. David's exuberance comes to a climax in this psalm's key verse: "Let the words of my mouth and the meditation of my heart," David exalted in verse 14, "be acceptable in Your sight, O LORD, my strength and my Redeemer."

Divinely inspired, David must have imagined God pulling a blank sheet of paper across His desk, designing everything we see around us. Its substance was shaped out of His own grandeur.

God molded this beautiful earth and said "Good!" seven times in Genesis, chapter 1. In Job we hear from God as He answered the troubled believer.

Who is this who darkens counsel
By words without knowledge?
Now prepare yourself like a man;

I will question you, and you shall answer Me.

Where were you when I laid the foundations of the
    earth?
Tell Me, if you have understanding.
Who determined its measurements?
Surely you know!
Or who stretched the line upon it?
To what were its foundations fastened?
Or who laid its cornerstone,
When the morning stars sang together,
And all the sons of God shouted for joy?

Or who shut in the sea with doors,
When it burst forth and issued from the womb;
When I made the clouds its garment,
And thick darkness its swaddling band;
When I fixed My limit for it,
And set bars and doors;
When I said,
"This far you may come, but no farther,
And here your proud waves must stop!"

Have you commanded the morning since your days
    began,
And caused the dawn to know its place,
That it might take hold of the ends of the earth,
And the wicked be shaken out of it? (38:2–13)

God was saying that it is He who has done all that and
more. And though Job questioned God—even blamed God
for his troubles, God found him without blame. Why?

Because Job believed all that God told him. Job believed that God is the God of the past, present, and future.

The creation of the world also tells us that God obviously delights in activity, color, beauty, wonder, and life, and much more. He made us. Why? Surely not for fun. We long for children out of our instinct for love, do we not? God made us that way. He is not only like that Himself, He *is* that. And being love Himself, God declared His presence in the past, present, and future through the book of 1 John 4:8–9: "He who does not love does not know God, for God is love," the book says. "In this the love of God was manifested toward us, that God has sent His only begotten Son into the world, that we might live through Him."

> God is the God of the past, present, and future.

The God of Yesterday and Today

Even with the evidence that God is the God of yesterday, today, and tomorrow, some still believe that the omnipotent Creator of man's first breath is passé. One writer has even authored a book saying that the figure of God withdrew from the Bible. But since Jesus came, God becomes more and more vivid in the Bible and in the world to this very day. It took 348 pages for that writer to put his theory together, but just one miracle to demolish the idea.

If anyone thinks God has dwindled, let him come to Africa. I've seen Him there—manifested in greater power than anywhere in the Old Testament—expelling demons, restoring the sick, healing the blind, curing the crippled, and making the deaf hear. The evidence of the power of God around us today is awesome. We continue to see every kind of wonder, miracles of healing, fantastic revelations of Christ by visions, dreams, providence, and miracles of answered prayer, of conversion, of provision, of guidance, of angelic protection, of gifts of the Holy Spirit, and of power over demonic forces.

These revelations will go on until Jesus comes again. But if it all stopped one hundred years from now, it would be looked back on with awe or incredulity. Some would say it was all merely a past phenomenon, and some would say it would never happen again. But one thing is evident. Today, we are in the midst of it as Israel was when faced with the Egyptians behind them and the Red Sea in front of them. Like many in Israel, the certainty is that many today actually have seen the display of God's awesome greatness, but crawl through life unimpressed, mistrustful, and fearful.

Future Tense Faith in a Present Tense World

One man with a message of past, present, and future faith was John the apostle. When he was up against the whole Roman Empire he wrote the marvelous and triumphant book of Revelation.

John was close to Jesus; it was a unique friendship. He also suffered for Christ. John was the man who saw what things meant. He read the signs with prophetic insight. What he saw was difficult to explain. Let's look at what he said: "Grace to you and peace from Him who is and who was and who is to come, and from the seven Spirits who are before His throne, and from Jesus Christ, the faithful witness, the firstborn from the dead, and the ruler over the kings of the earth" (Rev. 1:4–5).

Jesus' Witness of Himself

How can Jesus be a "faithful witness"? We are witnesses to Christ, but to what does Christ witness? This Scripture refers back to another passage, in John 8:13–18:

> The Pharisees therefore said to Him, "You bear witness of Yourself; Your witness is not true." Jesus answered and said to them, "Even if I bear witness of Myself, My witness is true, for I know where I came from and where I am going; but you do not know where I come from and where I am going. You judge according to the flesh; I judge no one. And yet if I do judge, My judgment is true; for I am not alone, but I am with the Father who sent Me. It is also written in your law that the testimony of two men is true. I am One who bears witness of Myself, and the Father who sent Me bears witness of Me."

Jesus witnesses to Himself. He said, "Let not your heart be troubled; you believe in God, believe also in me" (John 14:1). By His life and mighty deeds He has shown us who He is. He witnesses to who He is. **He is faithful to whom He told us He is and doesn't disappoint us.** If He were different now, He would not be a faithful witness. He is consistent with what He said and did. The life of Jesus spells hope for sinners and the sick and concern for everybody.

He is Faithful & doesn't disappoint!

Now, notice something. God backs up His faithfulness in this text in the words, "'I am the Alpha and the Omega, the Beginning and the End,' says the Lord, 'who is and who was and who is to come, the Almighty'" (Rev. 1:8). This is an unusual usage, for instead

> He is faithful to whom He told us He is and doesn't disappoint us.

of, "who is to come," we would have typically said, "who will be"—using the verb, "to be." God used "to be" twice in "who was, and is," then switched to a different verb and used, "to come." Why this peculiar way of putting it?

The reason is that **God** is "unusual." He **baffles grammar and syntax,** and the language has to be pushed around when we speak of Him. Christ Himself was a mystery, as He attests in Scripture: "All things have been delivered to Me by My Father, and no one knows the Son except the Father. Nor does anyone know the Father except the Son, and the one to whom the Son wills to reveal Him" (Matt. 11:27). To talk about Him in ordinary language always leaves something out.

The Lord's Language

When it comes to the Lord, human language is never good enough. The first Christians had to give new meaning to many words and even coin new words, because Jesus did new things and was a new kind of Person. God did not communicate about Himself

> God baffles grammar and syntax.

with mere words. He simply presented Himself with His actions, and to describe Him we often need a bigger and better language. When we speak of God, we often lack the words, sometimes feeling like the Queen of Sheba experiencing Solomon.

> And when the queen of Sheba had seen all the wisdom of Solomon, the house that he had built, the food on his table, the seating of his servants, the service of his waiters and their apparel, his cupbearers, and his entryway by which he went up to the house of the LORD, there was no more spirit in her. Then she said to the king, "It was a true report which I heard in my own land about your words and your wisdom. However I did not believe the words until I came and saw with my own eyes; and indeed the half was not told me. Your wisdom and prosperity exceed the fame of which I heard." (1 Kings 10:4–7)

God never relied on mere words to inspire our faith in Himself. To show us who and what He is, He *came!* "The Word became flesh and dwelt among us," the Gospel of John says, "and we beheld His glory, the glory as of the only begotten of the Father, full of grace and truth" (1:14).

God isn't a will be, could be, might be God, and He is not in the process of becoming something else. What He will be, He is now and always has been. God is the eternal unchanging One. "For I am the LORD," the book of Malachi says. "I do not change" (3:6).

But it is different for us as individuals. We are always finding something new in Him. Suppose you stand in a river at the water's edge. You are at the river, yet also the river keeps coming toward you. And the water we stand in will be the same water that somebody else may stand in tomorrow farther down-

> The God of Moses and Elijah is not behind us, but ahead of us.

stream as the river flows. God is like that. We come to Him. He is there, and yet He keeps coming to us. He is not just "being" God in some mysterious place.

Jesus Himself confirms this to us in the book of Luke: "I say to you, ask, and it will be given to you; seek, and you will find; knock, and it will be opened to you. For everyone who asks receives, and he who seeks finds, and to him who knocks it will be opened" (11:9–10).

The God of Moses and Elijah is not behind us, but ahead of us. You can't update Him. He has brought to us the dispensation of the Holy Spirit and has given us the wisdom to have faith in Him alone. And His promise to us is unwavering: "Trust in the LORD with all your heart, / And lean not on your own understanding," Proverbs says. "In all your ways acknowledge Him, / And He shall direct your paths" (3:5–6).

chapter 3

Your Way to a Faith Breakthrough

God plans for nothing to be ordinary and for none of His people to be worried or bothered by anything. Jesus pointed this out in many sermons to His disciples and to Israel.

In Matthew, chapter 6, for example, He admonished us that we—His people—are special and not to worry about anything:

> Therefore I say to you, do not worry about your life, what you will eat or what you will drink; nor about your body, what you will put on. Is not life more than food and the body more than clothing? Look at the birds of the air, for they neither sow nor reap nor gather into barns; yet your heavenly Father feeds them. Are you not of more value than they? Which of you by worrying can add one cubit to his stature? So why do you worry about clothing? Consider the lilies of the

field, how they grow: they neither toil nor spin; and yet I say to you that even Solomon in all his glory was not arrayed like one of these. Now if God so clothes the grass of the field, which today is, and tomorrow is thrown into the oven, will He not much more clothe you, O you of little faith? Therefore do not worry, saying, "What shall we eat?" or "What shall we drink?" or "What shall we wear?" For after all these things the Gentiles seek. For your heavenly Father knows that you need all these things. (vv. 25–32)

In the kingdom of God the extraordinary is so common it becomes customary, and each person is special. That's why God wants each and every one of us to trust Him. In that same teaching in Matthew 6, we learn what to do to get God's blessings as described above by Jesus: "But seek first the kingdom of God and His righteousness," Christ said, "and all these things shall be added to you" (v. 33).

> God plans for nothing to be ordinary.

The Fertile Ground

And in seeking His kingdom we must have faith, for faith is the fertile ground in which God moves. He plants qualities in the man or woman of faith, which soon become admired anywhere. Little people take on stature by faith in Christ. They have zest, a grip on life, and tackle difficulties with determination and confidence. It is common for believers to perform beyond their natural capacity. Jesus said to the unlearned fisher lads on the sea of Galilee, "Follow Me, and I will make you fishers of men" (Matt. 4:19). They switched direction and also elevation as they became His apostles.

But some say, "I'm not a faith person." If that's the case, there's bad news and good news. The bad news is that it's not scriptural. The Bible says, "Faith is the substance of things hoped for, the evidence of things not seen. . . . But without faith it is impossible to please Him, for he who comes to God must believe

> The road to faith is wide open and easily accessible to all.

that He is, and that He is a rewarder of those who diligently seek Him" (Heb. 11:1, 6). The good news is that we can all be "faith people." Faith is so vital that God intends nobody to be faithless. **The road to faith is wide open and easily accessible to all,** as Hebrews, chapter 10 says:

> Therefore, brethren, having boldness to enter the Holiest by the blood of Jesus, by a new and living way which He consecrated for us, through the veil, that is, His flesh, and having a High Priest over the house of God, let us draw near with a true heart in full assurance of faith, having our hearts sprinkled from an evil conscience and our bodies washed with pure water. Let us hold fast the confession of our hope without wavering, for He who promised is faithful. And let us consider one another in order to stir up love and good works. (vv. 19–24)

Of all that **faith** is, however, there is one thing that it is not: **It is not for the greedy. God, who made all the wealth** there is, is not against wealth, but those whose god is gold can expect no help from heaven.

Jesus' Parable of the Sower in Luke 8 is a prime example of how God warns us away from greed:

> A sower went out to sow his seed. And as he sowed, some fell by the wayside; and it was trampled down, and the birds of the air devoured it. Some fell on rock; and as soon as it sprang up, it withered away because it lacked moisture. And some fell among thorns, and the thorns sprang up with it and choked it. But others fell on good ground, sprang up, and yielded a crop a hundredfold. . . . He who has ears to hear, let him hear! (vv. 5–8)

Jesus continued, as He explained the meaning of the parable:

> The seed is the word of God. Those by the wayside are the ones who hear; then the devil comes and takes away the word out of their hearts, lest they should believe and be saved. But the ones on the rock are those who, when they hear, receive the word with joy; and these have no root, who believe for a while and in time of temptation fall away. Now the ones

> Faith is not for the greedy. God, who made all the wealth there is, is not against wealth, but those whose god is gold can expect no help from heaven.

that fell among thorns are those who, when they have heard, go out and are choked with cares, riches, and pleasures of life, and bring no fruit to maturity. But the ones that fell on the good ground are those who, having heard the word with a noble and good heart, keep it and bear fruit with patience. (vv. 11–15)

The same plain words address greed in the book of James:

Where do wars and fights come from among you? Do they not come from your desires for pleasure that war in your members? You lust and do not have. You murder and covet and cannot obtain. You fight and war. Yet you do not have because you do not ask. You ask and do not receive, because you ask amiss, that you may spend it on your pleasures. Adulterers and adulteresses! Do you not know that friendship with the world is enmity with God? . . . Or do you think that the Scripture says in vain, "The Spirit who dwells in us yearns jealously?" But He gives more grace. Therefore He says, "God resists the proud, but gives grace to the humble." (4:1–6)

Riches Mean Nothing in the End

A life whose chief aim is riches remains unfortunate because at the end of that life, you will have nothing. But it is eternal profit to follow God's directions: "Therefore submit to God," Scripture says. "Resist the devil and he will flee from

> A life whose chief aim is riches remains unfortunate because at the end of that life, you will have nothing.

you. Draw near to God and He will draw near to you. Cleanse your hands, you sinners; and purify your hearts, you double-minded.

Lament and mourn and weep! Let your laughter be turned to mourning and your joy to gloom. Humble yourselves in the sight of the Lord, and He will lift you up" (James 4:7–10).

Acting on Faith

The divine principle of faith is that as we act, God acts. We respond to Him by faith, and He responds to us for faith. Paul found that it operated like blood flowing through his

> The divine principle of faith is that as we act, God acts.

veins. "I have been crucified with Christ," Paul both lamented and boasted. "It is no longer I who live, but Christ lives in me; and the life which I now live in the flesh I live by faith in the Son of God, who loved me and gave Himself for me" (Gal. 2:20).

Faith, therefore, is a decision we not only must make, but act upon. **God doesn't want us to be like new gloves, uselessly waiting to be picked up off the shelf and slipped on.** Some pray, "Use me, O Lord," but then do nothing. There's the idea that being used of God means being another Luther, Wesley, or Tyndale. But we are alive to get on with the task at our elbow. That is all-important for us, for without action, nothing happens.

Action is an important principle of faith. Christ Jesus is alive in me. Many wait for the Spirit to move, but desire that He move in the direction they want. The moving of the Spirit is not just in our feelings. There's an often neglected yet thoroughly important verse in James 4:5 that says, "The Spirit who dwells in us yearns jealously."

> God doesn't want us to be like new gloves, uselessly waiting to be picked up off the shelf and slipped on.

The Holy Spirit within us conflicts with fleshly desire, urging us into service for Him. But it still requires our submission and our action, never losing fact that it all comes back to God's infinite mercy and grace.

For example, Ephesians says it best: "For by grace you have been saved through faith, and that not of yourselves, it is the gift of God, not of works, lest anyone should boast. For we are His workmanship, created in Christ Jesus for good works, which God prepared beforehand that we should walk in them" (2:8–10).

Having Just a Little Faith

Faith is a mutual act between God and us. This chapter is talking about two spirits in opposition—the spirit of the devil and the Spirit of God. They both pressure us. First, we read of the spirit who is now at work in those who are disobedient (Eph. 2:2). Then we read that when we are saved, we are created in Christ Jesus to do good works (Eph. 2:10). When we do His will, do His good works, it is by His grace. We can't pride ourselves on it. The glory is all the Lord's.

But what if some of us only have a little faith? Don't worry. Everybody starts there, or with no faith at all! Even the apostles were referred to as "Ye of little faith." If we are dissatisfied with ourselves, take heart, for the Spirit within us yearns, and He plans to strengthen us.

Faith Breakthrough

If we are poor believers, there can be a breakthrough. The whole Bible is written to break down unbelief and build up our fortifications of trust in God. We may study it intellectually for doctrine or for prophecy, but its central objective is to bring us the peace of perfect rest in God.

> Action is an important principle of faith.

The Bible consistently repeats the exhortation to trust in the Lord. **Every day brings changes in circumstances, and every day we need a reminder to trust Him.** Starting out weak, some biblical giants finally awoke to God, dared the impossible, and succeeded through faith in Him and by His glorious grace:

- Abraham, "father of all those who believe" (Rom. 4:11). Abraham believed God, and God counted it to him as righteousness, and he became the friend of God (James 2:23). Like everybody else, Abraham could have doubted. His own wife, Sarah, did and laughed at the promise of God as absurd. Abraham in Ur of the Chaldees was in terrible shape, possibly idolatrous. Faith came to him quite late in life, but it made him the most dominant character, aside from Christ, that the Middle East had ever known.

- **Jacob.** He was the grandson of Abraham. At the beginning, Jacob didn't even claim that he belonged to God. Then came a night when God wrestled with him, and Jacob experienced a breakthrough. It changed him so much that God changed his name to Israel (Gen. 32:28).

- **Gideon.** Gideon was a young and frustrated son of the local chief. He rose literally overnight to become a national leader. He began with very shaky faith, even complaining that God had done nothing. God nursed Gideon's faith, and eventually he faced an invading army five hundred times bigger than his own unarmed troops. But the Bible says he put to flight the armies of aliens. It was a classic operation of faith (Judg. 7).

- **Jehoshaphat.** He was a nervous king, not always pleasing to God. When he and the nation were in danger, God's Spirit fell upon a man in prophecy and it brought a breakthrough. Jehoshaphat's expectations soared, and again it led to a victorious episode in the annals of Israel (2 Chron. 20).

> Every day brings changes in circumstances, and every day we need a reminder to trust Him.

- **Thomas the Twin, better known as "Doubting Thomas."** He actually said, "I will not believe" (John 20:25). He was a practical-minded type, the kind who needs hard evidence, but even he experienced a faith breakthrough when he saw the risen Christ in his midst.

- <u>Seven downhearted disciples.</u> Seven men met on the beach of Galilee. Every one of them had failed miserably. They had faith and had seen miracles and demons cast out, but now they were far from any such scene. Their spiritual lives seemed to be finished. Then Christ came to them and recharged their batteries (John 21). Soon they set out on a venture that changed the whole known world—and it is now changing new worlds.

Praying for all the faithful in Christ Jesus who resided in Ephesus, the apostle Paul prayed for their own special kind of faith breakthrough:

That the God of our Lord Jesus Christ, the Father of glory, may give to you the spirit of wisdom and revelation in the knowledge of Him, the eyes of your understanding being enlightened; that you may know what is the hope of His calling, what are the riches of the glory of His inheritance in the saints, and what is the exceeding greatness of His power toward us who believe, according to the working of His mighty power which He worked in Christ when He raised Him from the dead and seated Him at His right hand in the heavenly places, far above all principality and power and might and dominion, and every name that is named, not only in this age but also in that which is to come. And He put all things under His feet, and gave Him to be head over all things to the church, which is His body, the fullness of Him who fills all in all. (Eph. 1:17–23)

Faith and Power

Notice that Paul never prayed for power. The New Testament never talks about a new infilling or another Pentecost. Paul prayed only that "the eyes of [their] under-standing [be] enlightened" (Eph. 1:18), that is, to see what resources lay at their very elbow. We pray for power when Christ has all power and has made His possession of power His Great Commission command. If He has all power, that's all that matters. It follows that as we obey His com-mand He will back us without our having to spend half our time begging Him to do so. The power breakthrough for the Ephesians was a faith breakthrough in realizing what was theirs already in Christ. We take it by faith, not through merit by the labors of prayer.

> As we obey His command He will back us.

Big Believers of Great Faith

We talk of "big believers" with "great faith." But some event had to inspire them and encourage them. They took their opportunity, changed their attitude, and believed. God honors such a holy resolve. Jesus commended one or two for their "great faith," but not one of them arrived at that happy posi-tion by a long and arduous process. They met Jesus. That was all and enough. Faith is just that—faith in Him. What Jesus commended was the quality of their faith, not the quantity of it. Ever-increasing faith is not some kind of trapeze act. It is as a little child who trusts his parents more as he grows older.

Courage in Living by Faith

Galatians 3:11 proclaims that "the just shall live by faith." But as we all know that's a tall order. To be sure, faith does involve taking a chance, or it wouldn't be faith. But taking a chance on God is hardly a gamble. He is faithful and sure. Faith, in reality, is confident anticipation based on the knowledge of who God is.

For example, Peter knew exactly who Jesus was, even that night the book of Matthew talks about, when Christ walked on the water. Jesus made His disciples get into a boat and go before Him to the other side, while He sent the crowd away who had gathered to see Him.

> When He had sent the multitudes away, He went up on the mountain by Himself to pray. Now when evening came, He was alone there. But the boat was now in the middle of the sea, tossed by the waves, for the wind was contrary. Now in the fourth watch of the night Jesus went to them, walking on the sea. And when the disciples saw Him walking on the sea, they were troubled, saying, "It is a ghost!" And they cried out for fear. But immediately Jesus spoke to them, saying, "Be of good cheer! It is I; do not be afraid." And Peter answered Him and said, "Lord, if it is You, command me to come to You on the water." So He said, "Come." And when Peter had come down out of the boat, he walked on the water to go to Jesus. But when he saw that the wind was boisterous, he was afraid; and beginning to sink he cried out, saying, "Lord, save me!" And immediately Jesus stretched out His hand and caught him, and said to him, "O you of little faith, why did you doubt?" And when

they got into the boat, the wind ceased. Then those who were in the boat came and worshiped Him, saying, "Truly You are the Son of God." (14:23–33)

Having faith means to act on the strength of what we know, expecting God to be to us what we know He is. When we "risk" everything on God, He proves to be faithful to what He has told us about Himself.

Faith is a leap into the light, not into the darkness. It is out of the unknown into the known, out of not knowing Christ Jesus into knowing Him. Believing is like a child who is in a situation where he could fall but who is without any fear because his father is waiting to catch him. Sometimes the child falls on purpose, fully expecting Dad to catch him.

> Having faith means to act on the strength of what we know.

So how much more valuable are we to our heavenly Father? Each of us is important to God, more than all the stars in the sky. He wants us to trust Him implicitly. He made us and will take pains with us. Faith allows Him to see us through until we rest in Him.

That also happens every time we experience or read about a miracle—it breaks through the unbelief of the world. It has to, or we could never get near to Jesus. Believe God! It will please some people and amaze everyone else.

Faith and Doubters

I met a youngster who challenged me by saying, "Preacher, you preach from a book that is two thousand years old. I'm only seventeen and don't want to live by such ancient rules.

I want to be modern, because I live today." It was noon and the sun was shining. I replied, "Young man, look at the sun. The sun is much older than two thousand years, yet I never heard anybody say 'I am cold because the sun is old!' The sun is old but very hot, and the Bible is old, but very powerful." He got the message.

Somebody else said to me, "I don't like the Bible because it is too old." I replied, "I don't mind how old a telephone directory is as long as it provides the correct numbers. Every time I read a Bible verse, I am getting through to the throne of God." Psalm 50:15 says, "Call upon Me in the day of trouble; / I will deliver you. . . ." God's lines are constantly open by His Word.

The Order of the Day

We are surrounded by doubters every day. Godlessness is the order of the day. Newspapers, radio, and television all push "irreligion and godlessness" down our throats for breakfast, lunch, and dinner. If we want faith, we should try a diet different from all the secular rationalization we are fed.

Feed on the Bible, prayer, Christian encouragement, and faith-building reading. Come hopefully, exercising faith, however nervously, and you will get more faith. The believer is destined to be a giant among pygmies, walking tall, riding high above the spiritual poverty of the world, the representative of a greater order of creation, a strength and a pillar for all to see.

> Feed on the Bible, prayer, Christian encouragement, and faith-building reading.

The Bible refers to believers as soldiers (2 Tim. 2:3). While it is true that we go through many battles in our Christian lives, I can't help but trust in God that we act as that Roman centurion did in the Gospel of Luke. The centurion's servant was sick and ready to die. When the soldier heard about Jesus, he sent elders of the Jews to Him, pleading with Jesus to come and heal his servant. Jesus agreed, but when He wasn't far from the house, the centurion sent friends to Jesus to tell Him the following:

> A true faith breakthrough is one that starts in our hearts and ends with God's answer to our need.

"Lord, do not trouble Yourself, for I am not worthy that You should enter under my roof. Therefore I did not even think myself worthy to come to You. But say the word, and my servant will be healed. For I also am a man placed under authority, having soldiers under me. And I say to one, 'Go' and he goes; and to another 'Come,' and he comes; and to my servant, 'Do this,' and he does it." When Jesus heard these things, He marveled at him, and turned around and said to the crowd that followed Him, "I say to you, I have not found such great faith, not even in Israel!" And those who were sent, returning to the house, found the servant well who had been sick. (Luke 7:6–10)

Faith in God never goes unnoticed by Him. **A true faith breakthrough is one that starts in our hearts and ends with God's answer to our need.**

Faith and Knowing

It seems that everyone is talking about faith these days, but what kind of faith is it and what are we placing our faith in? If someone plans on jumping out of an airplane, would it be more helpful for us to shout, "Don't be downhearted, just have faith," or "Don't worry! I packed your parachute carefully"?

Faith and Tomorrow

Some talk about having faith in the future. Just believe tomorrow will be perfect and wonderful. Why? For no known reason? That is just being hopeful and awfully brave because no one knows why the future should be any better than the present. In fact, the present isn't as good as the past in many ways.

Faith is trust, but tomorrow isn't something to trust in. All the tomorrows won't change and won't be brighter no matter how hard we want to believe it.

Some tell us to have faith in life. Creation is taken to be generally friendly. Life will treat us kindly. This could be the world's most common religion, with no creed and no one much to thank. It is not faith, but simply a psychological attitude of optimism without any support. Neither the Bible nor science gives it much encouragement. The reality is that the vast universe is hostile to human life. We live in this air bubble in the vacuum of space on a planet full of life in a lifeless void. In and of itself this is a daily miracle. Our preservation is an act of God's goodness, and that should encourage faith in Him, not in an all-powerful but kindly universe.

As it says in Scripture:

> Rejoice in the LORD, O you righteous!
> For praise from the upright is beautiful.
> Praise the LORD with the harp;
> Make melody to Him with an instrument of ten strings.
> Sing to Him a new song;
> Play skillfully with a shout of joy.
>
> For the word of the LORD is right,
> And all His work is done in truth.
> He loves righteousness and justice;
> The earth is full of the goodness of the LORD.
>
> By the word of the LORD the heavens were made,
> And all the host of them by the breath of His mouth.
> He gathers the waters of the sea together as a heap;
> He lays up the deep in storehouses.
>
> Let all the earth fear the LORD;
> Let all the inhabitants of the world stand in awe of
>   Him.

For He spoke, and it was done;
He commanded, and it stood fast. (Ps. 33:1–9)

The Truth About Faith

True faith means to place confidence in something. However, that does not mean that anything at all will do. Whatever we trust in must be trustworthy. Christian faith is faith in Christ— and that is not irrational. It is not a case of mere believing, because blind faith is careless and irresponsible, like putting your money into the hands of someone you don't know.

A friend told me his Christian brother felt sorry for people who had been in jail, and he employed men who had been in prison in order to give them a new start. He showed his confidence in one man by making him his general manager.

Later he discovered the man had been secretly robbing him, and his thefts almost ruined the business. He then learned that the reason for this trusted employee's previous sentence was embezzlement! Blind faith in anyone or anything will get us nowhere.

All over the world people are putting faith in an endless variety of religions, systems, gods, theories, sects, cults, and self-proclaimed messiahs.

The Wrong Kind of Faith

Only a fool would trust an unknown deity, but many do when they are influenced by strong emotional pressures and techniques. Some cults have committed, in recent times, mass suicide in their deluded hopes.

The vast majority of faiths, old as well as new, promise nothing this side of eternity. Their slogan might as well be "pie in the sky when you die."

The late Ayatollah Khomeini sent very young teenagers into minefields with the promise that if they died killing infidels, they would go straight to paradise. Logically, how can killing people make anybody fit for heaven? It is so grotesque and perverted, yet many did what he said. This is a prime example of the deceitfulness of satanic influence on earth.

> The vast majority of faiths, old as well as new, promise nothing this side of eternity.

By further example, the Spanish emperor at the time of the Inquisition was stricken with anxiety about his own salvation because he thought he had not burned enough Jews and others who were not Catholics!

Faiths are followed that bring nothing like the common experience of Christian believers. In fact, no real experience of God at all is experienced—no miracle, no forgiveness, no victory over sin, no strength in adversity, no peace with God, and no joy.

Some faiths, such as Islam, exalt resignation to fate as a great virtue. But Christianity does not. Christian believers overcome fate. They don't bow to the inevitable.

Following the Rules

The theology of most religions imposes rules. There are prayers to pray, practices to observe, and as a reward, offers of some kind of future hope. We may as well launch ourselves on a plank to cross the Atlantic as to launch our souls on untried religious systems to cross into eternity.

This is a day of suicidal fanaticism, violent assertion, screaming threats, and murder. Abraham, the father of three present-day religions, indulged in no raving demonstrations. In Christ's day, some who claimed to be children of Abraham fumed with hate and wanted to kill Jesus. He said: "If you were Abraham's children, you would do the works of Abraham. But now you seek to kill Me, a Man who has told you the truth which I heard from God. Abraham did not do this. You do the deeds of your father" (John 8:39–41). When the people he was talking to said, "We have one Father— God," Jesus replied:

> "If God were your Father, you would love Me, for I proceeded forth and came from God; nor have I come of Myself, but He sent Me. Why do you not understand My speech? Because you are not able to listen to My word. You are of your father the devil, and the desires of your father you want to do. He was a murderer from the beginning, and does not stand in the truth, because there is no truth in him. When he speaks a lie, he speaks from his own resources, for he is a liar and the father of it. But because I tell the truth, you do not believe Me. Which of you convicts Me of sin? And if I tell the truth, why do you not believe Me? He who is of God hears God's words; therefore you do not hear, because you are not of God." Then the Jews answered and said to Him, "Do we not say rightly that You are a Samaritan and have a demon?" Jesus answered, "I do not have a demon; but I honor My

Father, and you dishonor Me. And I do not seek My own glory; there is One who seeks and judges. Most assuredly, I say to you, if anyone keeps My word he shall never see death." (John 8:42–51)

Knowing the Truth

A psychiatrist once told me, "I don't believe that the Bible is the Word of God or that Jesus is the Son of God, but I am also a 'spiritual counselor.'" I now had become curious and replied, "Sir, how do you counsel people who are in despair? Suppose a couple comes to you whose marriage is on the rocks and whose hearts are bleeding. How would you 'counsel' them?" "Oh", he replied, "I just calm them down." I couldn't contain myself any longer and said, "Mister, a man on a sinking ship needs more than a tranquilizer. Don't calm him down, because he is going down already. A man on a sinking ship needs three things: rescue, rescue, and, again, rescue. When Jesus sees people in a shipwreck," I continued, "He doesn't throw them a handful of Valium pills with the words 'Perish in peace.' Instead His saving arm extends, reaching over the boiling abyss, gripping and lifting those hapless people. Christ then holds them with His powerful, nail-pierced hand and says, 'Because I live, you shall live also.'" Only Jesus saves; there is no Savior besides Him.

No Threats, No Swords, No Intimidation

People who know the truth don't get into a demented rage. When critics arise, they let the truth prove itself. The very method for spreading Christian truth shows what kind of gospel it is; no threats, no sword,

> The first Christians believed they could and would conquer the world by love, and they did.

and no intimidation are needed. Scripture confirms this. First Corinthians 1 says: "For the message of the cross is foolishness to those who are perishing, but to us who are being saved it is the power of God. For it is written, 'I will destroy the wisdom of the wise, and bring to nothing the understanding of the prudent.' Where is the wise? Where is the scribe? Where is the disputer of this age? Has not God made foolish the wisdom of this world?" (vv. 18–20)

The first Christians believed they could and would conquer the world by love, and they did. Today, we are commonly told to keep an open mind about religion. Never be dogmatic. That is the liberal view. It means we can never be sure. Of what use is religion then? It is supposed to assure us about the future and about God. If we keep an open mind about it, we brush aside all of Christ's wonderful promises and enjoy nothing at all that He assures us of.

Christians do *not* keep an open mind. They embrace the positive blessings of Christ. Their minds are settled, not open for review. Keeping an open mind about our journey through life is equally perilous. **We must know what our destination is and set our sights on it.**

> We must know what our destination is and set our sights on it.

The Bible does not encourage anybody to be dogmatic, but its language is always that of a sure and certain hope. For example, hope breeds spiritual assurance. In 2 Corinthians 1:6–7, Paul taught,

Now if we are afflicted, it is for your consolation and salvation, which is effective for enduring the same sufferings which we also suffer. Or if we are comforted, it is for your consolation and salvation. And our hope for you is steadfast, because we know that as you are partakers of the sufferings, so also you will partake of the consolation.

"We know" is a typical New Testament expression. Knowing that the sun will rise tomorrow makes us neither dogmatic nor arrogant. It is the simple attitude of Christians being sure of tomorrow and of God.

Who He Is and What He Does

What He has done, He will do; what He is, He will be. The common Christian testimony is likened to that of Paul: "I know whom I have believed," he said, "and am persuaded that He is able to keep what I have committed to Him until that Day [when Christ comes]" (2 Tim. 1:12b). That kind of certainty is no more than we would expect from any god worth calling God.

Yet, there is still hope for the unbelieving. Unbelief about God can be forgiven if people are truly about Him. The Bible itself says,

Therefore we must give the more earnest heed to the things we have heard, lest we drift away. For if the word spoken through angels proved steadfast, and every transgression and disobedience received a just reward, how shall we escape if we neglect so great a salvation, which at the first began to be spoken by the Lord, and was confirmed to us by those who heard Him, God also bearing witness both with signs and wonders, with various miracles, and gifts of the Holy Spirit, according to His own will? (Heb. 2:1–4)

The Unbelieving Believer

For example, a bishop went to a very talkative barber for a haircut. Having the churchman captive in the chair for fifteen minutes, the barber saw his chance. Aggressively, he announced he was a nonbeliever. The bishop then asked the barber, "Do you read the Bible?" "Me, read the Bible? Of course not. I'm a nonbeliever." "Do you read religious Christian books?" "You wouldn't catch me reading that rubbish. I'm a nonbeliever, I told you." "Do you ever go to church, or listen to TV or radio about God?" "You bet I don't!" "Have you any Christian friends that tell you about their religious experiences?" "No, thank you!" "What about anybody coming from a church to talk to you?" "These religion pushers know me! They dare not even knock at my door twice!" The bishop waited, smiling. "You understand now?" asked the barber. "Perfectly!" answered the bishop. "I understand that you are not a nonbeliever at all."

The barber retorted, "I tell you, I believe nothing." The bishop responded, "You can't be a nonbeliever. You don't even know what you are not believing. You can't disbelieve what you've never heard. I'll tell you what you are. You are a damned fool." The barber said, "Bishop, I'm surprised to hear you use language like that." The bishop replied, "I am not swearing. I'm quoting the Bible. It says, 'The fool hath said in his heart, There is no God,' and 'God shall send them strong delusion . . . that they all might be damned who believed not the truth.' You are an ignoramus about God and a fool for not wanting to know. So you are damned already."

Switching on Faith

We can't get away with ignorance or unbelief. They both have effects. Faith in God brings obvious benefits. It switches on the light. **Unbelief releases the acid of cynicism. You don't know what you believe.** "As they did not like to retain God in their knowledge, God gave

> Unbelief releases the acid of cynicism. You don't know what you believe.

them over to a debased mind" (Rom. 1:28). We would do better to ignore creation rather than the Creator.

Knowing God

God, however, isn't who some think He is. Paul the apostle said, "I know in whom I have believed." But it wasn't just anybody. Paul hated Christ and killed believers in Him until he met Him on that Damascus road:

> Saul [as Paul was called prior to his conversion], still breathing threats and murder against the disciples of the Lord, went to the high priest and asked letters from him to the synagogues of Damascus, so that if he

found any who were of the Way [Christians], whether men or women, he might bring them bound to Jerusalem. As he journeyed he came near Damascus, and suddenly a light shone around him from heaven. Then he fell to the ground, and heard a voice saying to him, "Saul, Saul, why are you persecuting Me?" And he said, "Who are You, Lord?" And the Lord said, "I am Jesus, whom you are persecuting. It is hard for you to kick against the goads." So he, trembling and astonished, said, "Lord, what do You want me to do?" Then the Lord said to him, "Arise and go into the city, and you will be told what you must do." (Acts 9:1–6).

From there Paul went into the city, evermore changed by the first experience with Jesus Christ, and became one of the most powerful disciples of the Lord.

Countless people have been like that—not looking for anyone to believe in and then meeting Jesus. **It is easy not to believe in Jesus when you don't know Him.** It takes no cleverness! But when Christ approaches or touches you, not believing is nearly impossible. No argument ever invented can nullify that experience.

> It is easy not to believe in Jesus when you don't know Him.

Meeting Jesus

The fact is that nobody can understand what it is like to meet Jesus until they do. Then they know why millions say, as Paul, "For to me, to live is Christ," or as John, "This is eternal life, that they may know You, the only true God, and Jesus Christ" (Phil. 1:21; John 17:3).

It has happened like that from the time He first appeared. The sex-obsessed woman of Samaria described in John 4 met Jesus for five minutes and couldn't get over it.

She roused the whole town in her excitement, and then when the men met Him, they felt the same. They didn't become religious enthusiasts. They became followers of Jesus, the Savior of the world, as they called Him. Modern Christians are like that too. They have found Him—the One who should come, whose presence makes heaven the place it is.

As wonderful as that first experience with God is, unless God allowed it, we could never know Him. **Only God can reveal God.** Many have spun God out of their rational thought, but their projections are about as heartwarming as an iceberg.

Scholars have worked on Jesus in the same way. They veil His face with unbelief and then call Him the Man nobody knows. They strip Him of what He is and then wonder what He is. They deny His miracles and His resurrection and reduce Jesus to their own lowest common denominator. He is too big for their logic, so they present Him as a miniature of who and what He really is.

> Only God can reveal God.

Nobody knows that Jesus. Believers know the Jesus whose face is the glory of God. It is a fact that human imagination is very limited and cannot reach God. We can only imagine something, as good as we know, not better. False gods are made in the image of men or women. "Eye has not seen, nor ear heard, / Nor have entered into the heart of man / The things which God has prepared for those who love

Him," Scripture says in 1 Corinthians 2:9. The experience of Christ is beyond those who are strangers to it.

Who God Is Not

Isaiah mocked those who tried to make images of their gods. Images are like gargoyles. Their character is usually as distorted as their appearance. The gods of the Greeks and Romans were lustful and treacherous. The early American tribes worshiped deities who demanded human sacrifices until the temple walls were coated inches thick with dried blood.

Even sci-fi writers' ideas of other life forms are usually ghastly nightmare figures. Every attempt to portray God comes up against the depravity of the human mind. In the same vein are the curious ideas circulating about heaven and how to get there. Our ideas come only from the Bible, and only the Bible has the right to tell us *how* to get there and *who* will get

> The more we understand that Book, the more our minds open to its revelations.

there. The Bible describes heaven as a place where only those cleansed in the blood of Jesus dare enter.

If we turn elsewhere to know God, we often feel nervous and depressed. The sacred writings of India, China, or Islam bring fear but little cheer. Open the Bible and a thousand rainbows of wonderful light stream out. **The more we understand that Book, the more our minds open to its revelations,** as flowers to the rising sun. The power that inspired it designed our souls to receive it.

The Creator who cares enough to let this human race continue obviously does not want to leave us in the dark about Himself. He reveals Himself. That is the only way we could know Him. Our hard reasoning is like flint that only makes sparks, not light. Isaiah 50:11 says: "Behold, all ye that kindle a fire, that compass yourselves about with sparks: walk in the light of your fire . . . [but] ye shall lie down in sorrow" (KJV).

Sparks and flashes of thought don't illuminate life's path very much. The philosophers are as lost as anyone and yet seek to guide us, like the blind leading the blind. God says, "Let there be light" (Gen. 1:3). He brought light to Abraham, Moses, David, the prophets, and finally through Jesus Christ, brings it to us through His Word, the Bible.

To get faith we all must read the Bible. It is self-proving. Its chemistry explodes and brings us confidence about what we are reading. Romans 10:17 explains exactly what faith is: "Faith comes by hearing, and hearing by the Word of God." Abraham believed God when God spoke. The Creator outfitted us with the power to recognize His voice, just as Abraham did.

And tied with hearing Him comes the ultimate promise from Christ Himself. "Most assuredly, I say to you," Jesus promised, "he who hears My word and believes in Him who sent Me has everlasting life, and shall not come into judgment, but has passed from death into life" (John 5:24).

The greatness of Christ's promise to us constitutes a fantastic incentive to vigorously read His Word and then proclaim it to those who are lost and cannot hear.

5

Faith, Prayer, and Promises

What is this faith I speak of? It is not a thing, a lump of something, an extra brain lobe, or something affixed to our soul. We *choose* to believe. Faith is an attitude!

Believers talk about and concern themselves with faith because it is the only basis possible for any workable relationship with God. It is delusion to expect dealings with God on any other terms. How else can an invisible God relate to us now and in the future? **If we can't trust the Almighty,** of all beings, **who can we trust?**

A Child's Faith and Prayer

A little girl was praying in her room, asking the Lord to give her a bicycle. The parents heard it and decided to act. But because of her young age they bought her a tricycle. When the child saw the tricycle she exclaimed, "Dear Lord Jesus, don't You even know what a bicycle is?" Yes, the Lord surely knew that, but He also knows that little girls who are not yet ready for a bicycle can get hurt on it.

The Issue of Faith

Faith is not certainty. It is a personal issue. Someone may have proven himself or herself up to now, but the future holds only personal assurances. We trust them because we know them. It is bound to be a matter of trust. If we thought they would change, we would not trust them. We read who God is in His Word. We may have proven Him to be true for ourselves up to this moment, but for the future we can do nothing else but trust Him.

> If we can't trust the Almighty, who can we trust?

The Bible says we are not to trust in weapons (Ps. 44:6), wealth (Ps. 49:6–7), world leaders (Ps. 146:3), man (Jer. 17:5), works (Jer. 48:7), or our own righteousness (Ezek. 33:13). But we are to trust in God's name (Ps. 33:21), His Word (Ps. 119:42), and in Christ. Matthew 12 says,

> The Pharisees went out and took counsel against Him, how they might destroy Him. But when Jesus knew it, He withdrew from there. And great multitudes followed Him, and He healed them all. And He warned them not to make Him known, that it might be fulfilled which was spoken by Isaiah the prophet, saying: "Behold, My Servant whom I have chosen, / My Beloved in whom My soul is well pleased! / I will put My Spirit upon Him, / And He will declare justice to

the Gentiles. / He will not quarrel nor cry out, / Nor will anyone hear His voice in the streets. / A bruised reed He will not break, / And smoking flax He will not quench, / Till He sends forth justice to victory; / And in His name Gentiles will trust." (vv. 14–21)

No faith is needed to believe that two plus two equals four, but life is a degree more complicated. Circumstances change like the ocean. The vastness of things affects the future. Obviously, what God might do is affected—He doesn't cut across events as if they didn't occur. He works no magic, turns no pumpkins into golden coaches. But He is all-wise and all-powerful, so much so that we have to leave things to Him to sort out. We look to Him, and that is something God takes into account. He made the world that way. Prayer and faith will enable Him to do what He could not otherwise do. No doubt it is true that God can do anything, but He doesn't do that without those who believe. That is His planned providence.

Faith, Promises, and Others

It is human nature to depend on the promises of others until we are disillusioned. Tricksters and con men feed on it. We trust people when they give us their word. We should be able to trust God, as He has given us His Word. A hundred generations have proven Him, and He has given us the same reason for relying upon Him, as well as express declarations of what He will undertake to do for us. And Scripture bears that out. **In the entire Bible, there are approximately 7,874 promises that God has made to us.** Many of the promises come in the form of a covenant.

Even though God won't act without our belief, trust, and faith in Him, He does a lot for us without our asking. "Your Father in heaven . . . ," Scripture says, "makes His sun rise on the evil and on the good, and sends rain on the just and on the unjust" (Matt. 5:45).

God is good, and good to all. Millions give Him no credit, though they are quick to blame Him when things that are not good hit them. The processes of nature seem unchangeable and regular. To this day, no one has shown that God has no part in this. **He keeps His promises** to the birds, the livestock, and all the wild animals—every living creature on earth (Gen. 9:9–10). God even gives us security for our harvest: "As long as the earth endures, seedtime and harvest, cold and heat, summer and winter, day and night will never cease" (Gen. 8:22 NIV).

> In the entire Bible, there are approximately 7,874 promises that God has made to us.

However, God has other good things for us. The promise is, "Seek, and you will find" (Matt. 7:7), for some good things are obtainable only by direct application. Actually, these are promised, and most of them are listed in Scripture, including: "No good thing does he withhold from those whose walk is blameless" (Ps. 84:11 NIV). When we come to the end of natural provision, Jesus said, "Ask, and you will receive" (John 16:24). "Everyone who asks receives. . . . If you then . . . know how to give good gifts to your children, how much more will your Father who is in heaven give good things to those who ask Him!" (Matt. 7:8, 11). If we ask for good, He will not send evil—ever! "Every *good* gift . . . comes down from the Father of lights," says James 1:17 (emphasis added).

The Exercise of Our Faith

The exercise of faith in prayer is a healthy activity. The bird in the nest must learn to fly and gather what is available. Having to ask is an excellent reminder to us of our dependency on God and is arranged to bring us to seek Him. It gives birth to a spirit of childlikeness, looking to our heavenly Father at all times. It is fellowship—family fellowship with our Father.

God certainly could have arranged to do everything for us, but the simplest understanding of human nature would bemoan the suggestion. No parent would be so irresponsible as to treat their offspring in that way. The object

> **He keeps His promises.**

is to lead a child to stand on his own two feet. God intends something very similar for us. His ultimate purpose is that we will not be just helpless dependents, like babes at the breast, but His coworkers in Christ Jesus.

His Gifts to Us

And to accomplish this, God, in His infinite wisdom and grace, has given us various gifts, described in 1 Corinthians:

> There are diversities of gifts, but the same Spirit. There are differences of ministries, but the same Lord. And there are diversities of activities, but it is the same God who works all in all. But the manifestation of the Spirit is given to each one for the profit of all: for to one is given the word of wisdom

through the Spirit, to another the word of knowledge through the same Spirit, to another faith by the same Spirit, to another gifts of healings by the same Spirit, to another the working of miracles, to another prophecy, to another discerning of spirits, to another different kinds of tongues, to another the interpretation of tongues. But one and the same Spirit works all these things, distributing to each one individually as He wills. (12:4–11)

These gifts are given to believers for the edification of the church, the body of Christ. **Every believer has been given spiritual gifts,** but the gifts belong to God and are given to be used for His glory.

Faith and Prayer

Prayer, however, is at present our sole access if we wish to be useful to God. It is so often forgotten that He actually created the kind of world in which prayer would be necessary.

Prayer was not an afterthought when the devil upset things. Even Jesus prayed. To help the ongoing affairs of the kingdom of God, prayer is essential. A lot goes on that God does not want, but we should pray that His will shall be done. We ask in prayer, *then* He performs. He planned that we should cooperate in this way, just as He planned to place Adam in the Garden of Eden to tend and keep it (Gen. 2:15).

> Every believer has been given spiritual gifts.

Prayer and promises go hand in hand. Jesus Himself explained that in the Gospel of John: "Most assuredly, I say to you, he who believes in Me, the works that I do he will do also; and greater works than these he will do, because I go to My Father. And whatever you ask in My name, that I will do, that the Father may be glorified in the Son. If you ask anything in My name, I will do it" (14:12–14).

We are His collaborators. The world and the people in it need care, and the promise that Christ will do whatever we ask is for the fulfillment of that purpose, not to get the moon or half a dozen Rolls Royce cars.

There are unconditional promises, such as the continuation of nature, but there's a great deal for which we must ask. As James 4:2 says, "You do not have because you do not ask." He is not going to spoon-feed us. He feeds the sparrows but does not throw food into their nests. If we want God to work, we must work in prayer. God does everything with prayer and nothing without it.

What Prayer Is

Prayer is the act of us speaking to God, not God speaking to us. God can speak to us any time He wants. He doesn't have to wait until we pray. In fact, no one in the Bible seemed to be praying when God spoke to them. God is close to us and can speak at all times, however it may be that we can't hear Him because we are clamoring for Him to say something.

Prayer is basically a time to pour out our hearts to Him. Listening, though, is also part of prayer. We should constantly be ready, for He can and will speak at any time.

It may seem strange to Christians today that there is nothing whatever in Scripture about praying to hear from God, for guidance, or anything else. There is plenty about hearing His voice, but almost nothing about waiting to hear. If we pray and wait to hear, when we do hear a voice speak, we need to know whose it is. The dangers are obvious. We must know His voice and the one sure way to do that is to read His Word and know Him.

The Voice of God

It is a sad fact of our nature—a psychological fact—that **our own desires can be so loud that they sound like divine commands.** Shout long enough about what we want to do, and the echo will come back sooner or later, but it is our own voice, not the voice of God.

People talk of how they wrestled with God over a decision. Looked at honestly, that is an invidious procedure. Is God like that? Hardly! In fact, they are wrestling with their own will, not God's. They want Him to agree. Do we really imagine we must wrestle with God to pry a secret out of Him about what He wants us to do? Surely He would just tell us without an all-out wrestling match.

After Jerusalem fell, many of the people wanted Jeremiah to inquire if they should leave the land. In their hearts they wanted to go to Egypt and meant to do so. They only wanted Jeremiah to persuade God to approve their plans. Jeremiah inquired, and God did not approve at

> Our own desires can be so loud that they sound like divine commands.

all. They went anyway, saying Jeremiah had lied about what God said. They ran into great trouble as a result. God had not said anything about their leaving in the first place. It is folly to make decisions in haste and to put words in the mouth of the Almighty.

There is a test for all "voices" and impulses—and that is the Word. For example, Isaiah warns, "If they speak not according to this word, it is because there is no light in them" (8:20 KJV). The Bible claims for itself the unique privilege of being the means through which God speaks.

He has nothing to say except through His Word, which may come to us through ministry or prophecy, which often we need, but personal directives never come through a third party. He tells no one else what you should do. There may be comfort, edification, and exhortation, but each of us is led of God if we are His children (Rom. 8:14).

What Is God Saying?

None of the great men and women in Scripture who heard God's voice were asking and waiting for it. God wanted to speak and did so. People often ask, "What is God saying to the church?" Why should God always be saying something to the church? Has He left us all in the dark about what He wants? There are spiritually superior persons who profess to know what nobody else knows, as if they were divine favorites who really stand before God as nobody else. The Spirit of the prophets is now the Spirit given to all believers. God reveals His secrets to His prophets, and we are all in that category today in Christ. When God speaks, it is a publicly broadcast message, not a telephone call.

If He has anything to say to the church as a whole, it is what Christ said when He left this world:

> Go into all the world and preach the gospel to every creature. He who believes and is baptized will be saved; but he who does not believe will be condemned. And these signs will follow those who believe: In My name they will cast out demons; they will speak with new tongues; they will take up serpents; and if they drink anything deadly, it will by no means hurt them; they will lay hands on the sick, and they will recover. (Mark 16:15–18)

Until that commission is completed God has no afterthoughts or overriding concern to get us involved in side issues, such as church structures and organization.

God has a revealed will. So, if we ask anything according to His will He hears us (1 John 5:14). That is why Christ gave us the petition "Your will be done / on earth as it is in heaven" (Matt. 6:10). Jesus said that if His words remain in us, "Ask, and it will be given to you" (Matt. 7:7).

The primary aim of prayer is not for our will to be done and not to persuade God to our way of thinking or force His hand. His expressed will is that men come to repentance. Everything in the New Testament spells that out clearly. If we ask according to that will, God hastens to answer. It is expressed in the prayer, "Your kingdom come. / Your will be done / On earth as it is in heaven" (Matt. 6:10). Nothing other than the gospel will achieve it.

To believe God when we ask, we must know we are heard and that we ask according to His Word, which is His revealed will. The Word of God lists many such instances:

We are told to pray, "Give us this day our daily bread" (Matt. 6:11). Jesus said, "Your heavenly Father [will] give the Holy Spirit to those who ask Him!" (Luke 11:13). He also said, "Tarry . . . until you are endued with power from on high" (Luke 24:49). We should ask for healing, for spiritual gifts, for one another, for those

> The primary aim of prayer is not for our will to be done.

in the assembly who sin, and for people in authority. These are all subsidiary requests heading up the greatest purpose of God—the world's redemption.

Faith and prayer are a single subject, dependent on each other. But there are requirements to consider. The Bible says there are personal stipulations attached to prayer.

For example, Psalm 66:18–19 stresses that we should pray with a purity of heart. Matthew 21:22 says we must believe in Jesus Christ as God, and 1 John 5:14 urges us to pray in accordance with God's will, which we find in His Word, the Bible.

But there is more. Jesus promises that "whatever things you ask when you pray, believe that you receive them, and you will have them" (Mark 11:24), but He also says that forgiveness is a major part of the Father answering those prayers. "And whenever you stand praying, if you have anything against anyone, forgive him, that your Father in heaven may also forgive you your trespasses" (Mark 11:25).

To have faith that God will answer our prayers is vital to our spiritual welfare. How wonderful it is that even as we pray, others benefit from our forgiveness and our Christlikeness! What a wonderful God we serve!

chapter 6

Faith: The Old and the New

There was a time when giants walked the earth. No, not literal giants, but men who by their faith stood head and shoulders above the rest.

These men, whose faith in God transcended mere belief, became legendary—men like Enoch, whom the Bible says "lived sixty-five years, and begot Methuselah. After he begot Methuselah, Enoch walked with God three hundred years, and begot sons and daughters. So all the days of Enoch were three hundred and sixty-five years. And Enoch walked with God; and he was not, for God took him" (Gen. 5:21–24); and Abraham, with whom God initiated the first of the unconditional theocratic covenants:

> Now the LORD had said to Abram
> [Abraham's former name]:
> "Get out of your country,
> From your family
> And from your father's house,

To a land that I will show you.
I will make you a great nation;
I will bless you
And make your name great;
And you shall be a blessing.
I will bless those who bless you,
And I will curse him who curses you;
And in you all the families of the earth shall be
blessed." (Gen. 12:1–3)

And finally, Samuel, who was dedicated to God before his birth and born in answer to his mother Hannah's prayer. This stalwart man of God heard God's call and was so bold as to call the entire nation of Israel to repentance. First Samuel 7 says,

Then Samuel spoke to all the house of Israel, saying, "If you return to the LORD with all your hearts, then put away the foreign gods and the Ashtoreths from among you, and prepare your hearts for the LORD, and serve Him only; and He will deliver you from the hand of the Philistines." So the children of Israel put away the Baals and the Ashtoreths [images of Canaanite goddesses], and served the LORD only. And Samuel said, "Gather all Israel to Mizpah, and I will pray to the LORD for you." So they gathered together at Mizpah, drew water, and poured it out before the LORD. And they fasted that day, and said there, "We have sinned against the LORD." And Samuel judged the children of Israel at Mizpah. (vv. 3–6)

The Ancients Who Knew God

These were the ancients—men who knew God intimately. They didn't use the word *faith,* as in a state of mind. They thought only in practical terms, as in walking with God, serving, fearing, obeying, and cleaving to Him. That is what faith is, and that is why **the Bible must be our guide every inch of the way.**

Today, sadly, faith is thought of as a possession, stacked safely somewhere in our psychological cupboard. We bring it out, dust it off, and exhibit it as occasion requires. The ancients would no more go through the day without faith than without their clothes. It was the atmosphere they breathed. However, the world thinks of religion as a mere topic of conversation, or occasional practice, with Sunday being the designated day to exhibit it. But for these great men, their relationship with God was the essential quality of all their waking hours. It was the very substance of their lives.

In biblical times the world was a perilous place. The nations had no idea how to handle sicknesses, plagues, droughts, and famines. Enemies surrounded them, hunted them, and killed them. But Israel learned from men of faith that God was "El Shaddai," their all-sufficient protector, deliverer, healer, stronghold, and shield.

Other nations looked to their gods—to the rain god if they wanted rain or to the god of fertility for their harvest. They offered a sacrifice at the shrines of those gods as a bribe when they wanted help. Pagans had no sustained sense of God's constant concern. Only Israel enjoyed that.

The Sheep of His Pasture

Concerning Israel, though, God sent the Bible prophets to assure His people of His faithfulness. He was their Shepherd, and they were the sheep of His pasture. This was far beyond heathen thought. Even the greatest of the unbelievers, such as Socrates or Aristotle, had no such divine awareness. Israel was truly God's chosen people.

> The Bible must be our guide every inch of the way.

The New Testament, though, introduced a faith of another kind. Surely the trust communicated by the Bible prophets continues there, but it is expanded beyond a physical covenant and takes in more than even the prophets who prophesied it understood. For example, Peter addressed this very subject to those in Pontus, Galatia, Cappadocia, Asia, and Bithynia:

> Of this salvation the prophets have inquired and searched carefully, who prophesied of the grace that would come to you, searching what, or what manner of time, the Spirit of Christ who was in them was indicating when He testified beforehand the sufferings of Christ and the glories that would follow. To them it was revealed that, not to themselves, but to us they were ministering the things which now have been reported to you through those who have preached the gospel to you by the Holy Spirit sent from heaven—things which angels desire to look into. (1 Peter 1:10–12)

Furthermore, the message of "holiness" was upheld,

linking the Old with the New Testament. "Therefore gird up the loins of your mind," Peter said, "be sober, and rest your hope fully upon the grace that is to be brought to you at the revelation of Jesus Christ; as obedient children,

> Jesus said the soul that sins is dead already.

not conforming yourselves to the former lusts, as in your ignorance; but as He who called you is holy, you also be holy in all your conduct" (1 Peter 1:13–15).

Jesus showed us that our physical dangers were not the all-important matter, nor was our material prosperity. The state of our real self, our personality or soul, was the all-important issue. The body would die, but how much worse it would be for the soul to perish. "The soul who sins shall die," Ezekiel 18:4 says, but **Jesus said the soul that sins is dead already,** and He comes as the resurrection and the life.

The first thought of the ancients had to be physical security and prosperity because they lived under threat against both. But they were wonderful believers. Their faith was not an easygoing belief in a creed, but it had to be exercised vigilantly as a daily shield against constant perils.

They pioneered true faith within a world that was entirely idolatrous. Whatever we trust God for, including eternal salvation, these old characters, under the most testing of conditions, show us how to believe. Their examples are recorded in Scripture because they afford vital guidance for all time.

Degrees of Faith

What we can glean from both the Old and New Testaments

is that there are varying degrees of faith. We may begin with a limited vision of what to trust God for or with only one prayer, "O God, help me." Succinctly, our faith may follow a process something like this:

1. *Believing that something is true.* The book of James reminds those who believe in one God that the devils also believe the same thing and tremble (James 2:19), which is not too encouraging! In John 11, Martha believed in the resurrection at the last day, but Christ wanted a faith that leaped to resurrection then and there. "I am the resurrection and the life," He said. "He who believes in Me, though he may die, he shall live" (v. 25). Similarly, the Jews believed their religion was true, though it did little for them because it never was in action. It is similar in these days. Faith may be no more than an agreement with a statement of truth, an intellectual assent. Believing simply that there is a God is not a saving faith, but it is a start.

2. *Believing that a person is genuine.* For example Nicodemus said to Jesus, "Rabbi, we know that You are a teacher come from God; for no one can do these signs that You do unless God is with him" (John 3:2). Jesus wanted a higher level of faith than being regarded simply as a teacher. He talked to Nicodemus about "believing" in a new way—a way that Nicodemus had never conceived. Many believed in Jesus as Nicodemus did—that He was a genuine man. But admiration can turn to commitment, as there is reason to think it did in the case of Nicodemus. However, just believing that Jesus is a good man is a fatal fallacy. A

good man would not be a liar, a deceiver, or crazy. Yet He claimed to be the Son of God. He was not a good man to claim such a thing, but a shocking blasphemer . . . unless it was true. If He was a good man, He must have been what He said—much more than a good man. In fact He would have to be exactly who He claimed to be—Christ, the Savior of the world.

3. *Believing in Jesus as an inspired person, such as a prophet.* In the book of Matthew, the disciples told Christ that people thought Him to be a prophet: "Some say John the Baptist, some Elijah, and others Jeremiah or one of the prophets" (16:14). For example, when He entered Jerusalem, "the multitudes said, 'This is Jesus, the prophet from Nazareth of Galilee'" (Matt. 21:11). They applauded Him, but Jesus, like Jeremiah, wept. They had gone so far but did not allow Him to take them under His wing and save them. We can't say He is a prophet. A prophet must be heard, and to hear Christ takes us a long, long way toward the ultimate spiritual goal—salvation through Him.

4. *Believing in God's power.* In Jerusalem, everyone believed in God's power. Many also believed in Christ's power. For instance, the Gospel of John says that "when He was in Jerusalem at the Passover, during the feast, many believed in His name when they saw the signs which He did. But Jesus did not commit Himself to them, because He knew all men, and had no need that anyone should testify of man, for He knew what was in man" (John 2:23–25). You see, people didn't doubt what they saw. He was a miracle

worker. They even wanted to make Him king. But Christ wanted a broader faith. They believed in His physical powers but did not place Him where He should be, as Lord and Savior. They asked Him for miracles, but He had more for them than to simply gratify their love of the sensational. Their faith was only in Him as a healer, which is worth little more than faith in a man as a doctor, driver, or even a plumber. We trust a doctor as a doctor only, not as a daily help. Christ is to be trusted for all things, not just a miracle or two. It is He who said,

I am the bread of life. He who comes to Me shall never hunger, and he who believes in Me shall never thirst. But I said to you that you have seen Me and yet do not believe. All that the Father gives Me will come to Me, and the one who comes to Me I will by no means cast out. For I have come down from heaven, not to do My own will, but the will of Him who sent Me. This is the will of the Father who sent Me, that of all He has given Me I should lose nothing, but should raise it up at the last day. And this is the will of Him who sent Me, that everyone who sees the Son and believes in Him may have everlasting life; and I will raise him up at the last day. (John 6:35–40)

5. *Believing as trust.* This turns faith into a personal relationship. We trust people, such as our parents. They know us and hold the key to our most confidential diary. We feel they won't fail us. That is the personal faith God wants us to place in Him. Our lives are as open to Him as if He sat in our living room. He knows

our past, present, future, and our most secret thoughts. And when we begin to trust Him to be our Father in heaven, that is the beginning of a saving faith. If we were trapped on a mountain ledge and an expert climber came to rescue us, we would simply have to put our lives in his hands, no matter how brilliant we were. When we take that same trust into the spiritual realm, it is a saving faith, and Christ is our Rescuer.

6. *Believing in Christ.* When we trust Christ in a way that we would never trust a close friend, this is real faith. The Bible says friends can let us down. "Even my own familiar friend in whom I trusted, / Who ate my bread, / Has lifted up his heel against me" (Ps. 41:9). Even our own parents may fail: "When my father and my mother forsake me, / Then the LORD will take care of me" (Ps. 27:10). It means surrender and let Him take over in all the areas of our lives.

That is how Paul wanted it to be for his converts. When he was giving instructions to Christians in the Thessalonian church, he told them their faith, hope, love, and perseverance in the face of persecution were exemplary. Then he concluded with a prayer. "Now," he said, "may the God of peace Himself sanctify you completely; and may your whole spirit, soul, and body be preserved blameless at the coming of our Lord Jesus Christ. He who calls you is faithful, who also will do it" (1 Thess. 5:23–24). **Christ can only save what we give to Him.** We must hand everything over to

> Christ can only save what we give to Him.

Him—body, soul, and spirit—for all time. Then He can do something for us. He doesn't want to save us piecemeal. Satan is the only rival for that kind of possession of us. But Christ gave His all, and we must give Him our all. That is the only true way to express our faith in Him.

What Faith Produces

Faith produces an interaction between Christ and me. It is also a catalyst, an element that brings about a change. **Believing is a relationship.** It is something alive and vibrant, affecting both myself and Christ. We find this so as Scripture guides us:

> His divine power has given to us all things that pertain to life and godliness, through the knowledge of Him who called us by glory and virtue, by which have been given to us exceedingly great and precious promises, that through these you may be partakers of the divine nature, having escaped the corruption that is in the world through lust. But also for this very reason, giving all diligence, add to your faith virtue, to virtue knowledge, to knowledge self-control, to self-control perseverance, to perseverance godliness, to godliness brotherly kindness, and to brotherly kindness love. (2 Peter 1:3–7)

The apostle Paul also recognized this truth and coined the reality of being a true believer and taking on the new nature as being "in Christ." For example, in 2 Corinthians 5:17 Paul said, "Therefore, if anyone is in Christ, he is a new creation; old things have passed away; behold, all things have become new."

Spiritually Transformed

Paul was describing the spiritual transformation that occurs within the inner man when a person believes in Christ as Savior. But there is also freedom. Romans 8:1–2 states, "There is therefore now no condemnation to those who are in Christ

> **Believing is a relationship.**

Jesus, who do not walk according to the flesh, but according to the Spirit. For the law of the Spirit of life in Christ Jesus has made me free from the law of sin and death."

The simplest faith in Christ has amazing effects. The simplest person can believe and enjoy the same effect as the wisest.

Jesus also looked for words. He had heard all the religious jargon of the scribes, which ordinary people couldn't appreciate or understand. But the common people heard Jesus

> **The simplest faith in Christ has amazing effects.**

gladly. He talked about faith but put it in the simplest of terms, such as: "Come unto Me," "Love Me," "Abide in Me," "Eat of Me," and "Follow Me!"

Faith is not one particular religious act. It is the transfer of responsibility for one's life totally to God when our own resources are inadequate. **Faith is a spiritual blending that makes us one with Christ.** It seems like such a simple concept, and it is. There is no other way by which we could possibly acquire all that Christ accomplished on the cross for us. We are saved by faith.

God's Character

One question, though, begs to be answered. And that answer matters far beyond anything we can think about. Before we can know what kind of God we place our faith in, we must ask ourselves what God's character is.

What is His nature or attitude? Is He good, easy, happy, vindictive, difficult, joyless? Is He the Great Critic, the hard-faced Judge? Does He care about us? Is He the unmoved Mover and indifferent to what goes on? What does He feel about our sins and our struggles? What is His makeup? **Our attitude about everything else will be revealed by what we think about God and who He is.**

Some great nations are what they are because of their religious ideas. In Europe and the West, Christian culture and tradition shape our minds differently from non-Christian peoples. So as Kipling once said, "Oh, East is East, and West is West, and never the twain shall meet, / Till Earth and Sky stand presently at God's great Judgment Seat." There are vast areas of oppression or freedom, of restriction or liberty, of advance or stagnation, coming directly from whatever notions of deities are common.

> Faith is a spiritual blending that makes us one with Christ.

Whatever effects stand present in this are only temporal issues, but our very souls are at stake, based on what we believe. The Bible addresses this point head-on and strikes directly at the heart of things as John the Baptist witnesses concerning Christ and who He is:

> He who comes from above is above all; he who is of the earth is earthly and speaks of the earth. He who comes from heaven is above all. And what He has seen and heard, that He testifies; and no one receives His testimony. He who has received His testimony has certified that God is true. For He whom God has sent speaks the words of God, for God does not give the Spirit by measure. The Father loves the Son, and has given all things into His hand. He who believes in the Son has everlasting life; and he who does not believe the Son shall not see life, but the wrath of God abides on him. (John 3:31–36)

Which God are we talking about, though? The word *God* is ambiguous. To what or whom does "God" refer? It is all a matter of character. Is He just merely something somewhere, shapeless in form, with a particular disposition?

The greatest thinkers can do no more than speculate. We can't spin God out of our own head. By reason alone, we could never know a human person. It is impossible, unless they open up to us. However, God naturally wishes us to know Him. He

> Our attitude about everything else will be revealed by what we think about God and who He is.

made us and wouldn't want His creatures ignorant of who He is. When we turn to the Bible, we have an impression of God so powerful that imagination has never matched it.

God is identified for what He is in Scripture in various situations. This is augmented in Deuteronomy 33:13–16. Moses, the greatest of Israel's prophets, was prophesying over the twelve tribes of Israel and declaring what they were and would become. He blessed Joseph and said,

> Blessed of the LORD is his land,
> With the precious things of heaven, with the dew,
> And the deep lying beneath,
> With the precious fruits of the sun,
> With the precious produce of the months,
> With the best things of the ancient mountains,
> With the precious things of the everlasting hills,
> With the precious things of the earth and its fullness,
> And the favor of Him who dwelt in the bush.
> Let the blessing come "on the head of Joseph,
> And on the crown of the head of him who was
>   separate from his brothers."

It was *that* God, the God of the burning bush, whom Moses wanted to come and bless Joseph. He described this visitation as God's favor. **God is the God of goodwill toward us.**

The angels that heralded the birth of Christ used the same word. In Luke 2:14, the angels announced the birth of Jesus to shepherds keeping watch over their flock by night, and proclaimed to them, "Glory to God in the highest, / And on earth peace, goodwill toward men!" That is God's attitude—goodwill toward men. We are the people of God's goodwill—people on whom His favor rests.

> God is the God of goodwill toward us.

The Goodwill of God

The premise of goodwill, though, is descriptive of God in a variety of other situations in the New Testament. For example, Hebrews 6:13–20 says:

> For when God made a promise to Abraham, because He could swear by no one greater, He swore by Himself, saying, "Surely blessing I will bless you, and multiplying I will multiply you." And so, after he had patiently endured, he obtained the promise. For men indeed swear by the greater, and an oath for confirmation is for them an end of all dispute. Thus God, determining to show more abundantly to the heirs of promise the immutability of His counsel, confirmed it by an oath, that by two immutable things, in which it is impossible for God to lie, we might have strong consolation, who have fled for refuge to lay hold of the hope set before us. This hope we have as an anchor of the soul, both sure and steadfast, and which enters the Presence behind the veil, where the forerunner has entered for us, even Jesus, having become High Priest forever according to the order of Melchizedek.

The same genial qualities describing God are dominant throughout the entire Bible—God's goodwill becomes common knowledge. When atheists argue, it is that kind of God they argue about, not Krishna, Buddha, or Allah. But Scripture clearly and thoroughly separates, describes, and distinguishes the God and Father of our Lord Jesus Christ from all other "gods."

The Holy Spirit, though, works in us what He worked in Christ. For instance, in Paul's letter to the Philippian Christians, he guided:

> Therefore, my beloved, as you have always obeyed, not as in my presence only, but now much more in my absence, work out your own salvation with fear and trembling; for it is God who works in you both to will and to do for His good pleasure. Do all things without complaining and disputing, that you may become blameless and harmless, children of God without fault in the midst of a crooked and perverse generation, among whom you shine as lights in the world, holding fast the word of life, so that I may rejoice in the day of Christ that I have not run in vain or labored in vain. (Phil. 2:12–16)

Moreover, Paul points to that very goodwill while addressing believers in Ephesus who were faithful in Christ Jesus:

> Blessed be the God and Father of our Lord Jesus Christ, who has blessed us with every spiritual blessing in the heavenly places in Christ, just as He chose us in Him before the foundation of the world, that we should be holy and without blame before Him in love, having predestined us to adoption as sons by Jesus Christ to Himself, according to the good pleasure of His will, to the praise of the glory of His grace, by which He has made us accepted in the Beloved. (Eph. 1:3–6)

The will of Him who dwelt in the burning bush was frightening. To release Israel, and to introduce the idea of freedom, God rocked Egypt and convulsed nature. Nothing could stand in His way—not Pharaoh, armies, gods, rivers, seas, or Israel's ingratitude and reluctance. They seemed to want to hug the chains that had bound them, but that was unacceptable for God. He wanted the very best for His people.

That is His character—goodwill—ready to turn the world right side up, even by tearing the Son of God from His own bosom to come to earth to fulfill His wishes for the benefit and blessing of the unworthy sons of men.

The Name of Yahweh

Israel had a name for God that was so holy they avoided even using it. In the Bible it is translated "the Lord," but in the original Hebrew it is Yahweh. The Scripture used by Jesus was Greek and called God "Lord" (Greek, *kurios*). *Lord* is a common and ordinary word.

> **"Yahweh" meant that God was separate, One on His own, "holy."**

The awesome name *Yahweh* was never used in the New Testament. It is always *Lord,* even when quoting the Old Testament.

For centuries experts have tried to find where the great name of Yahweh came from. They suspected that it had been used previously by other Eastern peoples, but could not verify it. The name Yahweh was unique, used only in Israel. Divine revelation filled it with an awesome and profound meaning. The names of heathen deities were never like that. **Yahweh,** in fact, **meant that God was separate, One on His own,** "holy."

As a matter of fact, numerous biblical passages refer to God as being unlike anyone or anything. A case in point is one of many instances when King David praised God:

> For Your word's sake, and according to Your own heart, You have done all these great things, to make Your servant know them. Therefore You are great, O Lord GOD. For there is none like You, nor is there any God besides You, according to all that we have heard with our ears. And who is like Your people, like Israel, the one nation on the earth whom God went to redeem for Himself as a people, to make for Himself a name—and to do for You great and awesome deeds for Your land—before Your people whom You redeemed for Yourself from Egypt, the nations, and their gods? For You have made Your people Israel Your very own people forever; and You, LORD, have become their God. Now, O LORD God, the word which You have spoken concerning Your servant and concerning his house, establish it forever and do as You have said. So let Your name be magnified forever, saying, "The LORD of hosts is the God over Israel." And let the house of Your servant David be established before You. For You, O LORD of hosts, God of Israel, have revealed this to Your servant, saying, "I will build you a house." Therefore Your servant found it in his heart to pray this prayer to You. And now, O Lord GOD, You are God, and Your words are true, and You have promised this

goodness to Your servant. Now therefore, let it please You to bless the house of Your servant, that it may continue before You forever; for You, O Lord GOD, have spoken it, and with Your blessing let the house of Your servant be blessed forever. (2 Sam. 7:21–29)

First Chronicles 17:20 also repeats that there is none like the Lord, and Psalm 86:8 reverberates that among the gods there is none like the Lord of lords. The name of the Lord is exalted on high in Jeremiah 10:6–7, repeating that God's name is great in might and holiness. His name is evermore inexpressible.

The name of the Lord is not a mere label. Moses asked God what His name was (Ex. 3:13). He already had heard His name, but what was it when revealed? Even Abraham knew it, but God "made known His ways to Moses" (Ps. 103:7). Moses was asking what God's name signified.

Moses realized that the God who was sending him to Egypt was more than he had ever thought when he used His name. Knowing the name of Yahweh, as knowing the name of an ocean, says nothing about its mysterious depths. God was more awesome than Moses had ever dreamed. He was told to take off his shoes when facing the burning bush (Ex. 3:5) because the presence of God makes the desert sand holy. He is "the Lord." There are many gods, but only one Yahweh. There is no category of gods that includes Him. He is set apart.

Some pronounce *Yahweh* as "Jehovah." Isaiah 43:10 says that Israel is witness to Yahweh (or Jehovah). Jesus said His witnesses are His disciples (Acts 1:8). The Christian witness has always been the fact that Jesus Christ is Lord. The name of Jesus is now the highest title in heaven and earth, the name of the King of kings. But this supreme name conveys more than God's being holy and awesome. He became incarnate, suffered, died, and was raised again for unworthy mortals. His title, "Lord," signifies more than the Old Testament "Yahweh." It also signifies God as He made Himself known in Christ, the final revelation.

We find, then, that the character of God is one of concern, goodwill, and action. The Lord God of Israel and our Lord Jesus Christ did greater things than ever before, and Jesus continues to perform ten thousand wonders every hour of every day.

Confirming His deity, Jesus said, "My Father has been working until now, and I have been working" (John 5:17). He has rivals, but they can't compete. His character outshines all that has ever been pictured in men, women, or myth.

The character of God is therefore also seen in Christ and in His gospel. The gospel stands alone, and His glory proves matchless. Vast multitudes come to Christ because their own religions offer so little. The gospel of Christ offers everything. Signs accompany it as do wonders, marvels of salvation, conversions, and miracles of healing. His light and truth lighten the future and illuminate eternity. Evil spirits are expelled. Christ gives immunity to spells and curses and all the works of the devil (1 John 3:8). We worship the Supreme God of all gods; millions recognize that fact.

> The faithfulness of God is the great mark of the divine character.

If we are going to be full of faith, then God must be faithful. **The faithfulness of God is the great mark of the**

divine character. The Old Testament people exalted in the Lord for His "faithfulness" and sang of it in the Psalms. We don't read of ancient Israelite people having faith, but they are described as trusting God or calling upon Him and obeying Him. The word *faith* was applied to the Lord—He kept faith with His people.

Never Changing

The faithfulness of God means that He doesn't change from what He said He was. He is faithful in Himself. He never deviates from what He has been—a God of integrity, always Himself, constantly the same. Whatever He did, it was always consistent with what He was. He never did anything out of character. Whatever He did was of Him. That faithfulness meant people could trust Him at every stage of their lives.

This has tremendous implications for Christian believers. What He was when He went to Calvary and hung on the cross, and when He was jeered by enemies, and when He rose again, that is He. That is Jesus. It always was and always will be. He is "the Lamb slain from the foundation of the world" (Rev. 13:8), and He is the same Lamb John saw seated on the throne of glory.

> Today, He is still the same Christ.

Today, He is still the same Christ. His love did not burn out in that one great effort of those bitter hours. It did not exhaust His goodwill. What He did on the cross is what He is now. What He was, bleeding and torn and riveted with iron to the wooden cross, He is now, crowned with glory and seated upon the central throne of all creation.

He is the same One who dwelt in the burning bush, the God of goodwill. The character of our God is incomparable. The God of faithfulness is the One whom we can trust to do for us nothing but good. That is what He is. There are none beside Him and none like Him.

chapter 7

Faith and God's "I Will"

The phrase "I will" occurs about four thousand times in Scripture. It is a common expression used frequently by many people, not just by God. The curious thing, though, is that in the Bible God says it far more often than everyone else put together.

Through the lips of the Old Testament prophets the Lord constantly says, "I will," but it becomes a special feature emphasized in many passages. In Exodus, God uses the phrase "I will" 96 times, but the same words are used by others only 22 times, and what they declare they will do is referred to only 32 times. God's use of it is so frequent that it sets up the Bible as the Word and the will of God.

These are some very significant Bible facts. In chapter 9 of Genesis we have the first example of God's special use of "I will." Between verses 9 and 17, God uses an expression like "I will" eight times. God deals with us all on such terms. Our part is to believe.

Then the prophecy of Isaiah represents God speaking and using "I will" in almost every chapter. In chapters 41 and 46 He says, "I will" 46 times. Through the lips of Jeremiah the prophet, God says, "I will" hundreds of times. We read it in 49 chapters out of the 52, and in chapter 30 God says, "I will" 28 times.

God Always Will

The New Testament is similar. In the Gospels, Jesus constantly says what He will do, but little is made of what anyone else says, which to some extent is unusual. The Gospels do highlight special cases when people said, "I will," and then couldn't, wouldn't, or didn't. Perhaps the most famous illustration is found in the book of Matthew. Jesus and the chosen twelve were having their Last Supper together when the Lord said to them,

> "All of you will be made to stumble because of Me this night, for it is written: 'I will strike the Shepherd, and the sheep of the flock will be scattered.' But after I have been raised, I will go before you to Galilee." Peter answered and said to Him, "Even if all are made to stumble because of You, I will never be made to stumble." Jesus said to him, "Assuredly, I say to you that this night, before the rooster crows, you will deny Me three times." Peter said to Him, "Even if I have to die with You, I will not deny You!" And so said all the disciples. (26:31–35)

Peter and the others told Jesus, "I will not deny You," but they did. The devil told Jesus,

> "For what is your life? It is even a vapor that appears for a little time and then vanishes away."

"All this authority I will give You," but he never did. Jesus spoke about a son who said, "I go," but didn't; and his brother who said, "I will not," but went (Matt. 8:19; 26:35; Luke 4:6; Matt. 21:28–30).

The book of James makes "I will" quite an issue. Chapter 4 teaches that faith produces dependence on God:

> Come now, you who say, "Today or tomorrow we will go to such and such a city, spend a year there, buy and sell, and make a profit"; whereas you do not know what will happen tomorrow. **For what is your life? It is even a vapor that appears for a little time and then vanishes away.** Instead you ought to say, "If the Lord wills, we shall live and do this or that." But now you boast in your arrogance. All such boasting is evil. Therefore, to him who knows to do good and does not do it, to him it is sin. (vv. 13–17)

For James, it was what God wills, not what we will that takes effect. In other words, **it is not our "I will" but God's "I will."**

Christ came to fulfill the Father's "I will." Therefore His will is supreme. The scribes' teaching was what other scribes and scholars had passed down through the generations. The academics of today are very similar. Most of their teaching is quotation of other scholars.

Unless theologians quote theologians they are not considered sufficiently informed; their authority is built on one another. It seems that their work is to consider what every other scholar has said and then give their own judgment as to who is right. The teachers of Christ's day did the same, but Jesus spoke on His own original authority. His words were, "Amen! Amen! I say to you."

> It is not our "I will" but God's "I will."

Jesus said, **"Heaven and earth will pass away, but My words will by no means pass away"** (Mark 13:31). Therefore, God's "I will" will never pass away. The words and the "I Will" of Jesus are for all. His revelation is not private but is written as part of the Word of God to us all.

Similarly, in the beginning of creation He spoke (Gen. 1:3; John 1:1–3). He said, "Let there be light," and there is light to this day. His command endures and makes the sun work the way it does. His Word is the most real thing of all. His will is

> "Heaven and earth will pass away, but My words will by no means pass away."

good, merciful, positive. That is the very essence of His revelation about Himself. Jesus said, "I will," to one sufferer on behalf of all sufferers.

Christ does the will of the Father, and, like the Father, He is the great "I will" God. This paints a picture of our God with His face open and love shining upon us. What a light upon our rugged path through life! "I will" characterizes God all the way through Scripture. He says to mankind, "I will."

This same "I will" is the phrase used at the marriage altar by a bride and bridegroom when they commit themselves to each other. It is as if the Almighty stood at the marriage altar and committed Himself with the same words. Isaiah, the great prophet, alluded to this when he proclaimed,

> "For your Maker is your husband,
> The LORD of hosts is His name;
> And your Redeemer is the Holy One of Israel;
> He is called the God of the whole earth.
> For the LORD has called you
> Like a woman forsaken and grieved in spirit,
> Like a youthful wife when you were refused,"
> Says your God.
> "For a mere moment I have forsaken you,
> But with great mercies I will gather you.
> With a little wrath I hid My face from you for a
>   moment;
> But with everlasting kindness I will have mercy
>   on you,"
> Says the LORD, your Redeemer. (Isa. 54:5–8)

He is never sullen, unwilling, unyielding, nor reluctant, but when we come to Him, His face is open. All that is needed is that His people be willing.

Being a Volunteer

Psalm 110 shows us how to act and what to strive for:

> Your people shall be volunteers
> In the day of Your power;
> In the beauties of holiness, from the womb of the
>   morning,
> You have the dew of Your youth.

The LORD has sworn
And will not relent,
"You are a priest forever
According to the order of Melchizedek."
The Lord is at Your right hand;
He shall execute kings in the day of His wrath.
He shall judge among the nations,
He shall fill the places with dead bodies,
He shall execute the heads of many countries.
He shall drink of the brook by the wayside;
Therefore He shall lift up the head. (vv. 3–7)

God's "I will" is always positive, but of the fifty-four references in Exodus to what people will do, most are negative, what man will *not* do. God doesn't say what He will not do. For example, look at Exodus 3. God was speaking to Moses about delivering Israel out of Egypt:

Thus you shall say to the children of Israel: "The LORD God of your fathers, the God of Abraham, the God of Isaac, and the God of Jacob, has sent me to you. This is My name forever, and this is My memorial to all generations." Go and gather the elders of Israel together, and say to them, "The LORD God of your fathers, the God of Abraham, of Isaac, and of Jacob, appeared to me, saying, 'I have surely visited you and seen what is done to you in Egypt; and I have said I will bring you up out of the affliction of Egypt to the land of the Canaanites and the Hittites and the Amorites and the Perizzites and the Hivites and the Jebusites, to a land flowing with milk and honey.'" Then they will heed your voice; and you shall come, you and the elders of

Israel, to the king of Egypt; and you shall say to him, "The LORD God of the Hebrews has met with us; and now, please, let us go three days' journey into the wilderness, that we may sacrifice to the LORD our God." But I am sure that the king of Egypt will not let you go, no, not even by a mighty hand. So I will stretch out My hand and strike Egypt with all My wonders which I will do in its midst; and after that he will let you go. And I will give this people favor in the sight of the Egyptians; and it shall be, when you go, that you shall not go empty-handed. But every woman shall ask of her neighbor, namely, of her who dwells near her house, articles of silver, articles of gold, and clothing; and you shall put them on your sons and on your daughters. So you shall plunder the Egyptians. (vv. 15–22)

Notice how the chapter spotlights God's positive goodwill, and then the human attempt to oppose it and negate it. But God comes back at it with His persistent positive, overcoming the human negative.

Declaring His Will

The Bible is the Word of God to declare His eternal will. What He did tells us what He would do and what He is. There would be little point in telling us what His will was if it wasn't the same anymore. It would then have only historical or academic interest. But it is not mere history. The Bible is here to show what God is throughout all ages, and Scripture upholds that.

The book of 1 Chronicles gives evidence in David's praise psalm:

Glory in His holy name;
Let the hearts of those rejoice who seek the LORD!
Seek the LORD and His strength;
Seek His face evermore!
Remember His marvelous works which He has done,
His wonders, and the judgments of His mouth,
O seed of Israel His servant,
You children of Jacob, His chosen ones!
He is the LORD our God;
His judgments are in all the earth.
Remember His covenant forever,
The word which He commanded, for a thousand
    generations,
The covenant which He made with Abraham,
And His oath to Isaac,
And confirmed it to Jacob for a statute,
To Israel for an everlasting covenant,
Saying "To you I will give the land of Canaan
As the allotment of your inheritance,"
When you were but few in number,
Indeed very few, and strangers in it. (16:10–19)

Faith sees God as Lord of eternity. Time does not affect Him, but it affects everyone and everything else. **God is not a figure of past history. In Him everything is present.** In glory He is the crucified One, the Lamb of God.

The Essence of Faith

The absolute essence of faith is to accept God today to be what He was yesterday. We have no other grounds for trust except that He will keep faith with us. He will not be one thing today and another thing tomorrow. He is not temperamental. He made one revelation, forever about Himself. If He does not live up to it, then the revelation is worthless. But His name is faithful and true. In the book of Revelation, Jesus instructed John the Apostle as to what message to bring to the various churches. "And to the angel of the church of the Laodiceans write," Jesus said, "'These things says the Amen, the Faithful and True Witness, the Beginning of the creation of God'" (Rev. 3:14).

> God is not a figure of past history. In Him everything is present.

God not only *is* something. We only know what He is by what He *does*. He is a God of activity. A Christian cannot believe in fate. To have faith in God means to have faith in a God who acts, who answers prayer, who performs wonders, and who is, in fact, Supreme.

Read what He was, and believe what He is. When people take the Bible and expect God to bless them, answer their prayers, prosper them, heal them, work miracles, and save them, that is faith as the Bible knows it. They have struck the keynote of Scripture.

When God says, "I will," it forms a covenant. We can take the book of Genesis, chapter 9, as an example of this covenant. Known as the Noahic Covenant, it is the third general or universal covenant and is considered significant in revealing God's love and unchangeable ways:

> So God blessed Noah and his sons, and said to them:
> "Be fruitful and multiply, and fill the earth. And the
> fear of you and the dread of you shall be on every

beast of the earth, on every bird of the air, on all that move on the earth, and on all the fish of the sea. They are given into your hand. Every moving thing that lives shall be food for you. I have given you all things, even as the green herbs. But you shall not eat flesh with its life, that is, its blood. Surely for your lifeblood I will demand a reckoning; from the hand of every beast I will require it, and from the hand of man. From the hand of every man's brother I will require the life of man. Whoever sheds man's blood, / By man his blood shall be shed; / For in the image of God / He made man. / And as for you, be fruitful and multiply; / Bring forth abundantly in the earth / And multiply in it." Then God spoke to Noah and to his sons with him, saying: "And as for Me, behold, I establish My covenant with you and with your descendants after you, and with every living creature that is with you: the birds, the cattle, and every beast of the earth with you, of all that go out of the ark, every beast of the earth. Thus I establish My covenant with you: Never again shall all flesh be cut off by the waters of the flood; never again shall there be a flood to destroy the earth." And God said: "This is the sign of the covenant which I make between Me and you, and every living creature that is with you, for perpetual generations: I set My rainbow in the cloud, and it shall be for the sign of the covenant between Me and the earth. It shall be, when I bring a cloud over the earth, that the rainbow shall be seen in the cloud; and I will remember My covenant which is between Me and you and every living creature of all flesh; the waters shall never again become a flood to destroy all flesh. The rainbow shall be in the cloud, and I will look on it to remember the everlasting covenant between God and every living creature of all flesh that is on the earth." And God said to Noah, "This is the sign of the covenant which I have established between Me and all flesh that is on the earth." (vv. 1–17)

The Spontaneous God

This covenant is a solo resolution, without a second party. It is unilateral. But it is *for* a second party. It is made for Noah and his sons and descendants, and also for the birds and wild creatures who could not make any agreement with God. It contains no "proviso" and lays down no terms.

It is important to see that God's "I will" covenants have two qualities. They are spontaneous and they are absolute. No one pressed God for **the covenants,** and they stand firm without any condition. Such covenants **are a sheer act of grace and concern from start to finish.** Jesus said, "Have faith in God" (Mark 11:22). Leave things to Him. He does all things well.

The Gospel of Matthew records thirteen instances of Christ's using the words, "I will." These thirteen are not the full complement of what He will do, but He speaks in the same way as the Lord God of the prophets and stands as the Son by the side of His Father as the great "I will."

> The covenants are a sheer act of grace and concern from start to finish.

Most of Christ's claims relate to the immediate present, not some far-off future. He said, "Come to Me . . . and I will give you rest" (Matt. 11:28); "The one who comes to Me I will by no means cast out" (John 6:37); "I will make you fishers of men" (Matt. 4:19).

Each claim is backed by His veracity alone. **Jesus** never tries to convince people of what He said. He **doesn't argue.** His words are enough, and if believed, they prove themselves. There is no other proof required:

> Behold! My Servant, whom I uphold,
> My Elect One in whom My soul delights!
> I have put My Spirit upon Him;
> He will bring forth justice to the Gentiles.
> He will not cry out, nor raise His voice,
> Nor cause His voice to be heard in the street.
> A bruised reed He will not break,
> And smoking flax He will not quench;
> He will bring forth justice for truth.
> He will not fail nor be discouraged,
> Till He has established justice in the earth. (Isa. 42:1–4)

We believe entirely on His authority, and His authority is undeniable, unmistakable. Jesus, when talking to the Pharisees, didn't mince any words. On one occasion, in the Gospel of John, He was assertive and matter-of-fact: "I am the light of the world. He who follows Me shall not walk in darkness, but have the light of life" (8:12). The Pharisees argued with Jesus and told Him that he bore witness of Himself and His witness was not true. So Jesus retorted,

Jesus doesn't argue.

> Even if I bear witness of Myself, My witness is true, for
> I know where I came from and where I am going; but

you do not know where I come from and where I am
going. You judge according to the flesh; I judge no one.
And yet if I do judge, My judgment is true; for I am not
alone, but I am with the Father who sent Me. It is also
written in your law that the testimony of two men is
true. I am One who bears witness of Myself, and the
Father who sent Me bears witness of Me. (8:14–18)

They asked Him where His father was, and Jesus told
them,

"You know neither Me nor My Father. If you had
known Me, you would have known My Father
also." These words Jesus spoke in the treasury, as He
taught in the temple; and no one laid hands on Him,
for His hour had not yet come. Then Jesus said to
them again, "I am going away, and you will seek Me,
and will die in your sin. Where I go you cannot
come." So the Jews said, "Will He kill Himself,
because He says, 'Where I go you cannot come'?"
And He said to them, "You are from beneath; I am
from above. You are of this world; I am not of this
world. Therefore I said to you that you will die in
your sins; for if you do not believe that I am He, you
will die in your sins." (8:19–24)

There is a tremendous "I will" in John 14:16. It is unconditional and inevitable, a sheer, unsolicited act of the divine
will. "I will pray the Father, and He will give you another
Helper, that He may abide with you forever." He did not say,
"If you pray." Christ said, "I will pray." The disciples did not
pray for it. The Day of Pentecost was not the result of a
church's beseeching God and prevailing in perfect unity as is

so often suggested. It was the sovereign act of Christ and the Father, independent of all human action.

It was also a fulfillment of the "I will" of God in Joel 2:28: "I will pour out My Spirit on all flesh." God's outpoured Spirit is not a matter of the will of men and of their desires and prayers. The Comforter has come. There is no need to pray, "Lord, rend the heavens and come down." *He is here!* Nothing is needed but faith to act. We can safely rest in the assurance, the established fact, that the Spirit of God is with us.

> We believe entirely on His authority, and His authority is undeniable, unmistakable.

Today's God

The Lord has fulfilled His promise in the twentieth century. Some parts of the church attempted to stop what was happening. They had even prayed for revival but opposed the form in which it came. In Berlin, scores of Protestant churches declared it to be "from below" when God did pour out His Spirit. In Britain, the great biblical expositor Dr. G. Campbell Morgan, a man greatly appreciated by Pentecostal believers, was heard to say that what they testified to was "from the pit of hell."

> The believer is on the side of the inevitable.

But God said He would pour out His Spirit, and nothing could stop Him. He has and is doing so. Now, a major section of the worldwide church has plunged into the river flowing from the throne.

Christ said, "I will build My church." He has. He is doing so. He will complete it. **The believer is on the side of the inevitable.** He walks with victory. He faces the dawn, not the darkness. The kingdom is coming.

chapter 8

The Faith of Abraham

The battles that most changed the world have been listed by historians, but it was rightly said that the greatest of them was fought in the heart of Abraham. If anyone thinks of Abraham as just a Bible character, they have not even begun to understand the world in which he lived and, as a result, the world in which we live.

The Bible names him more than three hundred times, but because of his faith his name is inscribed upon the whole of the Middle East and upon world history to this day.

Faith That Changes

He was the first man noted for his obedience of faith. His life's career was consistent with that faith. Abraham believed God, and it was counted to him as righteousness. **What is of faith is forever.**

Faith changes men, who, in turn, change the world. Abraham was the man who began the civilizing process fifteen hundred years before the Greeks and Romans. The Pharaohs were in Egypt one thousand years before Abraham and continued another two thousand years after him, but they affected the world less than he did. The Pharaohs left no moral mark and only cluttered the desert sands with colossal monuments to their own egos. Abraham left not one single physical trace behind him for us to see. But all of our lives today, religious or not, are different because of who and what he was.

> What is of faith is forever.

Abraham was not deeply religious. In the modern, contemporary sense he wasn't religious at all. He had no creed, no hymns, no Bible, no images, and no theology. But he knew God personally. He walked with God and was God's friend (2 Chron. 20:7).

To this patriarch, God wasn't a go-to-church-once-a-week obligation, pushed into the spare corner of life. There was no church to attend. He didn't believe God just to be faithful to tradition. There was no tradition. God was his way of life. Like money or sport is to half the world today, God was to Abraham.

Faith on Course

Abraham didn't believe in order to save his own soul. His faith was neither a ticket for a joyride to heaven nor an insurance policy to escape hell. He came from Ur of the Chaldees and knew their pagan myths, but Abraham was starting on a new learning course. His tutor was the Lord. The nations had developed crude and cruel superstitions for themselves. Abraham threw himself upon God. To carry on without God wasn't an option.

Abraham believed God for two reasons. First, he found that there was a living God. Second, the only sensible thing to do was to carry out what God said. His faith changed the future, but that is not why he believed. He never dreamed of any such mission. In fact, he forsook the world and got as far away as he could from the world as it was. He changed it by leaving it. He believed God simply because God was there. That must still be the most rational thing anybody can ever do.

Astronaut Neil Armstrong stepped on the moon on July 20, 1969, and said that his one small step was a giant leap for mankind. Far bigger for mankind was the step Abraham took when he left Ur of the Chaldees. He was the pioneer of walking by faith in God and with God.

Abraham began life in wealthy Ur of the Chaldees and then moved to Haran. After that, he sacrificed his fine dwelling for a black goatskin tent in the wild, moorland scrub of the Negev. He moved around only with his family, shepherds, and cattlemen much like a Bedouin sheik. Secretly in his heart he nourished the ideal of a new way of life—a life full of the fullness of God. The Bible says he searched for such a place. "He waited for the city which has foundations, whose builder and maker is God" (Heb. 11:10).

When Abraham began the life of a tent dweller, a petty king plagued the countryside—an adventurer chief called Chedorlaomer, who was akin to a Mafia godfather. For twelve years, he extorted tribute—protection money—from the little nearby communities. Five city-states rebelled against Chedorlaomer and his supporting chieftains, but that only provoked him to worse deeds. This gangsterlike crew set out on a wholesale plundering expedition. In his rampage, he overwhelmed Sodom, Gomorrah, Zeboim, and Bela, the notorious cities of the plain.

Now Lot, the nephew of Abraham, lived at Sodom. He, his wife, and his married daughters were all taken captive, and the raiders plundered everything they had. Abraham heard this and decided to do something about it. He had made friends with strong-arm leaders in the area, and they joined him. It represented a well-trained and substantial private force. They pursued the chiefs in a well-organized rescue operation. Under Abraham's leadership they overthrew Chedorlaomer and his whole gang and brought back the captives unharmed, as well as everything they had pillaged, and a little extra as compensation booty.

The king of Sodom himself was rescued and went out to meet Abraham at the Valley of Shaven after his return from the defeat of Chedorlaomer and the kings who were with him. The book of Genesis explains it further:

> Then Melchizedek king of Salem brought out bread and wine; he was the priest of God Most High. And he blessed him and said: "Blessed be Abram of God Most High, / Possessor of heaven and earth; / And blessed be God Most High, / Who has delivered your enemies into your hand." And he gave him a tithe of all. Now the king of Sodom said to Abram, "Give me the persons, and take the goods for yourself." But Abram said to the king of Sodom, "I have raised my hand to the LORD, God Most High, the Possessor of heaven and earth, that I will take nothing, from a thread to a sandal strap, and that I will not take any-

thing that is yours, lest you should say, 'I have made Abram rich'—except only what the young men have eaten, and the portion of the men who went with me: Aner, Eshcol, and Mamre; let them take their portion." (14:18–24)

God showed him that the city he looked for, which God would build, would not enrich itself at the expense of others, by devastation. Abraham saw a better way.

Back then, cities lived by destroying each other and looting the harvests and wealth and using captives as slaves. The whole idea of military strength was to plunder. For example, Judges 5 gives the account of the Canaanite uprising against Israel, which Deborah subdued. It describes the mother of the Canaanites leaning out of the window and being told, "Are they not finding and dividing the spoils: a girl or two for each man, colorful garments as plunder for Sisera, colorful garments embroidered, highly embroidered garments for my neck—all this as plunder?" (v. 30 NIV). When Abraham rejected the practice, it baffled the greed of the king of Sodom.

God's Servant

Abraham knew he had acted as God's servant and felt that he had no need to deduct his own salary from the results. God confirmed His approval. "The word of the LORD came to Abram in a vision, saying, 'Do not be afraid, Abram. I am your shield, your exceedingly great reward'" (Gen. 15:1). Abraham believed God. He saw that with such a God he need not kill and slaughter and strip other people of their possessions to enrich himself in marauding raids; God would look after him. Abraham's faith led him to two new principles: First, the strong should help the weak, not take advantage of them, and second, faith in God meant that you did not have to create mayhem.

God could make you rich without making others poor. That was the new ideal. For long centuries, it was an ignored ideal, considered hopelessly impractical. **The world** is very slow to learn such lessons. It **prefers to work on the principle of the survival of the fittest,** push the weak to the wall, do the best for yourself no matter who goes under. This is not the Bible's way.

Lot, Abraham's nephew, was typical, always thinking about how he could benefit and be richer, smarter, or better than anyone else. However, a situation arose with Lot and Abraham. He and Abraham were men of substance with extensive herds—the wealth of the

> The world prefers to work on the principle of the survival of the fittest.

day. They needed good pastures. This led to quarrels and even fights between the herdsmen and shepherds of Lot and Abraham. It could have led to bloodshed and a permanent rift between uncle and nephew.

But Abraham valued good relationships more than material gain. He made a goodwill gesture to Lot that was amazing and generous. Lot could take what he wanted, and Abraham would take anything that was left. Abraham knew Lot and fully understood that he would take the best. He knew that he could not shame his avaricious nephew.

Lot certainly acted as expected. He took the best, choosing the most fertile area. Genesis describes it as "well watered" and "like the garden of the LORD" (Gen. 13:10). Lot was well pleased with himself. Not only had he obtained the richest pastures, but cities were close by that would serve as quick markets for his business.

One of these cities was Sodom, already notorious for its wickedness. But for the sake of good business, Lot became a leading citizen. The New Testament says that Lot was a righteous man who was distressed by the filthy lives of lawless men. He lived among them day after day and was tormented in his righteous soul by the lawless deeds he saw and heard (2 Peter 2:7–8).

> Abraham's love for and faith in God gave him wisdom beyond all borders.

But Lot chose to stay there just the same because there were good business pickings. The Bible phrase describes it as "loving the world."

Abraham was not an intellectual, but he had knowledge of God and yearned to be with Him. Scripture says, "The fear of the LORD is the beginning of wisdom; / A good understanding have all those who do His commandments" (Ps. 111:10). And **Abraham's love for and faith in God gave him wisdom beyond all borders.**

Searching in Vain

Men of genius would burst upon the world scene in the distant future. They would cast their nets of thought far and wide, seeking knowledge and understanding. They would invent new ways to live and new ways to rule cities. But they were destined never to know what Abraham knew. Their searching missed the ultimate discovery: to know God and to realize that understanding God does not come from earthly wisdom. Paul said that earthly wisdom was useless in understanding God:

> Where is the wise? Where is the scribe? Where is the disputer of this age? Has not God made foolish the wisdom of this world? For since, in the wisdom of God, the world through wisdom did not know God, it pleased God through the foolishness of the message preached to save those who believe. For Jews request a sign, and Greeks seek after wisdom; but we preach Christ crucified, to the Jews a stumbling block and to the Greeks foolishness, but to those who are called, both Jews and Greeks, Christ the power of God and the wisdom of God. Because the foolishness of God is wiser than men, and the weakness of God is stronger than men. (1 Cor. 1:20–25)

God would never wish to be unknown. Abraham picked up a golden key marked "faith." By it he opened heaven. Men of genius are as rare as icicles in summer. Abraham was not one of them. **God** is not the chairman of an exclusive club for intellectuals, but He **keeps His front door open for anyone.** He

> God keeps His front door open for anyone.

would never deprive Himself of the love of the millions in preference to the one-in-a-million prodigy.

The suggestion that we must not believe if men of intellect do not is a very nonintellectual assumption. If we had to find Him via a labyrinth of learning, He would have very small company around Him. To have the love of the vast masses of mankind, the means had to be different. He makes Himself known to those who look up to Him in childlike hope.

Learning to Trust

Abraham learned to trust God, and this trust revealed to him the paths of peace. His eyes scanned far horizons indeed. He was the first to discern the paths of righteousness, paths in the sea, and ways in the wilderness. The paths of righteousness and peace have been found. They are marked and known. Used or not, they can never be forgotten. If we traced them back, they would bring us to the tent door of Abraham, where God said to him, "Walk before Me and be blameless" (Gen. 17:1).

Why, though, did God speak to Abraham? It came from God's side, not Abraham's. God has shown concern for the world. When nobody sought Him, He sought them. Abraham was not seeking God. He made Abraham aware of who He was and gave him simple instructions to leave Ur. He was not told where to go, but he went. Thus began an unforgettable life. Hebrews 11:8–10 describes it and noted that Abraham lived in tents away from houses and streets. Why? To get paganism and city manners and customs out of his system. Abraham had been born and bred in an idolatrous civilization. God was to purge him of everything except what He showed him. He showed him he had a destiny beyond his own interests and in the future of nations. God said, "I will make you into a great nation and I will bless you . . . and all peoples on earth will be blessed through you" (Gen. 12:2–3 NIV). **Abraham was the first man of a new world order.**

Faith for Today

But why do we have faith today? To bless ourselves? To get wealth and be prosperous? If we have such faith, God gave it. But He enriches us to enrich others and to pass on the blessings we have been given. Politicians produce manifestos and agendas looking after their own corner of the world, but what is the purpose of a nation? Just to exist with no moral aims? Individuals have their own also, but what about their life purpose? Abraham lived on that level.

> Abraham was the first man of a new world order.

Faith, though, is the divine passport to God's very best. For example, we said that God planted Abraham in an unfriendly wilderness. God also planted the church in an unfriendly world, with the same purpose as that of Abraham.

When Jesus sent out His disciples, He gave them a divine passport into every land on earth. "Go into all the world and preach the gospel to every creature," Jesus commanded. "He who believes and is baptized will be saved; but he who does not believe will be condemned" (Mark 16:15–16). Christ was following the will of His Father expressed to Abraham, "I will bless you . . . And you shall be a blessing. . . . And in you all the families of the earth shall be blessed" (Gen. 12:2–3). They could forget about saving themselves. He would look after that. Their concern must be to save mankind.

The Mission at Hand

The Great Commission commits us to a mission, which continues Christ's mission. It is the reason for a church and gives it the right to exist. Concerned only with itself, it is purpose-less in God's eyes and harmless to hell. Faith only operates when linked with God's purposes, and the first of them is to bless all families of the earth.

Sometimes, though, faith in God is in itself an act of courage. For instance, the strangest episode in Abraham's life was his call to sacrifice his son, Isaac. By faith Abraham, when God tested him, offered Isaac as a sacrifice. He who had received the promises was about to offer his one and only son, even though God had said to him, "It is through Isaac that your offspring will be reckoned" (Heb. 11:18 NIV). Abraham rea-soned that God could raise the dead, and figuratively speak-ing, he did receive him back from death (Heb. 11:19).

> Faith is the divine passport to God's very best.

It might shock us that Abraham would even contemplate human sacrifice. The four thousand years' distance makes it impossible for us to understand a man of his time. Human sacrifice was common and was practiced more than three thousand years after Abraham, as in Central America. Abraham was the learner and beginner of faith in God. Spiritual lessons percolate very slowly into our human understanding.

God never meant Isaac to be sacrificed, but God tested Abraham on his own cultural level. Such a practice was then an expression of extreme religious devotion. He learned, in fact, that God wanted no offering of human blood. The pur-pose of this episode was the same as all God was doing with Abraham—to create a new culture in which bloodshed had no place.

From Abraham, it passed into the Hebrew tradition when everyone around continued such sacrifices. The voice of God at the most dramatic moment stopped Abraham's hand. He had exhibited incredible faith. All his expectations were that Isaac would be the father of generations and nations. To be willing (right or wrong) to sacrifice him showed staggering trust in the Lord. As we read in Hebrews, Abraham believed that God could raise his only son, Isaac, from the dead if necessary. God drew Abraham's road map, and he rarely left it. He was God's man traveling on God's highway.

It was not uncommon at that time for men to use the name of their god as part of their own name. Pharaoh Tutankhamen's god was Ahmun. It is thought that Abram took God's name as part of his own and made it Abraham, translated "the (divine) father is exalted."

However something happened that was far more significant. God took Abraham's name as part of His name! He called Himself the "the God of Abraham"! The Almighty identified Himself with a man.

A New God

It meant that the reputation of God rested on Abraham. What God was like—new God to the world in general—would be assumed from what Abraham was like. God risked His name by joining it with Abraham.

Abraham believed in the Lord, and the Lord believed in Abraham. Something similar is reflected in what Jesus said in Matthew 10:32, "Whoever acknowledges me before men, I will also acknowledge him before my Father in heaven" (NIV).

That's the inner truth about **faith.** It is not merely an agent for getting things or doing things or being something.

It **relates us to God.** Faith is fellowship and is always the condition for our relationship with God. He puts faith in our hearts, and then He puts His faith in us to do His will. It is "the faith of God."

Unless that faith is there, God has no faith in us. That is how it appears from John 2:23–24: "Many believed in His name. . . . But Jesus did not commit Himself to them." The words *commit Himself* are the same as *believe.* Their faith was not right, and Jesus knew it. But when

> **Faith relates us to God.**

faith is right, Jesus *does* "commit Himself" to us. Imagine that! Christ coming to us in trust! The whole business of God's promises, dealings, association, and relations with us becomes possible once this mutual trust is established.

If Jesus identifies Himself with us and says, "I am the Jesus of Reinhard Bonnke" or "I am the Jesus of Anni Bonnke" **we should act like it!**

Abraham was what God made him, and a credit to this day, and God was what Abraham made Him appear to be. Despite Abraham's imperfections, a child of his times in many ways, God shone through, a God worth knowing. Abraham was what he was because of what his God was—His qualities, values, greatness, virtues. God did not choose Abraham because of his

> **If Jesus identifies Himself with us we should act like it!**

perfection but because of His own. God transmitted what He was to Abraham through his faith. The process that began in Eden was restarted with Abraham, God making man in His own image.

The Purpose of Faith

The purpose of faith is for the process to continue. "When He is revealed, we shall be like Him, for we shall see Him as He is" (1 John 3:2).

Of all that faith is and has in store for he that believes, there is one thing it does not have. Faith, to be sure, has no elbows. In all groups, there are those alert to seize the main chance, steal the show, who elbow others aside and occupy the front position. In contrast, there is a man to admire in Acts 1—a man called Joseph or Barsabas, who was also called Justus. He must have had remarkable humility and godliness. Justus was one of two men chosen as candidate to fill the vacancy among the twelve apostles left when Judas committed suicide. They cast lots on this occasion—we would say that they tossed a coin for it. It came down heads for Matthias. We never hear of Justus again in Scripture.

What jealousy could have embittered him for the rest of his life! He seems to have been a disciple of John the Baptist and followed Christ from the very beginning. Now he had been thrust aside. He was not to be a member of the most illustrious group of men ever to walk on earth! But there was never a single hint that he took offense or disturbed the church by any resentment. There are legends about his later career, which reflect nothing but credit upon him. It was thought that this Joseph, or Justus, was one of the seventy disciples whom Jesus had sent out, and he is said to have been the one to carry the gospel to Ethiopia.

How? He was a man of faith who knew that the Lord was on his side. When a man or woman has faith in God, the honors of men don't matter. They leave such issues in the hands of the Lord. Papius records that the pagans tried to poison this humble man, but he miraculously survived. A man who has such trust in God that he carried no poison in his spirit was unlikely to become the victim of a poisoned chalice.

Lot, however, was another story. He never understood why Abraham allowed his business sense to be overruled by his principles of faith in God, and who lost his social opportunities by staying away from the cities. Lot perhaps thought his uncle was a fool. Someone must be in the forefront, but it is a question of whether we desire personal honor or faith. Jesus said, "How can you believe, who receive honor one from another?" (John 5:44).

Choosing the Lifestyle of Faith

Abraham chose faith, and honor was added. Lot did nothing for the cities. But Abraham the man of faith did. He fought for them, rescued their captured citizens, and begged God not to destroy them. Sodom eventually was destroyed. We read this remarkable comment in Genesis 19:29: "God remembered Abraham, and sent Lot out of the midst of the overthrow." Lot was delivered for the sake of Abraham!

Abraham rescued Lot two times. Lot finished up living in a cave with his two incestuous daughters, who had children by him, their morals corrupted by the evils of Sodom. He had earlier offered them to the will of a sex-crazed mob as a substitute for two male visitors the Sodomites wanted so they could have sex with them (Gen. 19:5).

And concerning his wife, Jesus said, "Remember Lot's wife" (Luke 17:32). Like her daughters' husbands, she also could not tear herself away from the city life, in contrast to

Abraham who forsook cities with his view filled with the vision of the city of God.

They all cynically ignored the warnings of angels and perished. The very ground of Sodom exploded upward and fell in sulfuric salts from the skies. Lot's wife was caught in the suffocating fumes and the salts coated her like a pillar. This is a prime biblical example of the results of having no faith.

Remaining behind, Abraham believed that God was making all things come together for good. He believed God's word to him, "I am your . . . exceedingly great reward" (Gen. 15:1). No strain and anxiety about loss or gain. He had God—El Shaddai, "the Enough God." He didn't want to have what God didn't want him to have.

God fulfilled the promise to Abraham to make of him a mighty nation. He could afford to let Lot take the best pasturage. The Lord said to Abraham after Lot parted from him, "Lift up your eyes from where you are and look north and south, east and west. All the land that you see I will give to you and your offspring forever. I will make your offspring like the dust of the earth" (Gen. 13:14–16 NIV).

Lot had a small area but no divine covenant. While drunk he fathered a family by his daughters that grew into sworn enemies of Israel. Everything to which he sold his soul to accumulate wealth went up in the smoke of Sodom and Gomorrah. Archaeology locates the possible site as beneath the waters of the Dead Sea.

Jesus put the principle of Abraham into His famous promise of the Sermon on the Mount, Matthew 6:33, "Seek first the kingdom of God and His righteousness, and all these things shall be added to you." Furthermore, He taught us not to worry about life: "Do not worry about tomorrow" (Matt. 6:34).

Jesus was thinking of the same blessing of Abraham that God said would bless all families. "Your heavenly Father knows" (Matt. 6:32)—you don't need to remind Him or ask.

In contrast, look at how money is viewed today. Big business now puts the love of money before the love of people. The "downsizing" principle in business today leaves the majority unsure and depressed about their future and their jobs. It is a vast social evil, which breeds general uncertainty. That is bad for business. Putting money before people begins a downward spiral. Abraham was blessed because he lacked the money motive. Jesus said, "Wisdom is justified by her children" (Matt. 11:19).

Even though some may believe it, faith is not a facility for getting more than enough. The Bible says, "If we have food and clothing, we will be content with that. People who want to get rich fall into temptation and a trap" (1 Tim. 6:8–9 NIV). "Keep your lives free from the love of money and be content with what you have, because . . . we say with confidence, 'The Lord is my helper'" (Heb. 13:5–6 NIV).

God and Private Gain

Private gain—to have more than enough—was never the use to which Bible believers put their faith. Nevertheless, faith creates conditions in which we can prosper according to God's purpose, since God knows our hearts. If God wants a multimillionaire, He makes one, and no doubt does so for the kingdom of heaven's sake.

God never promises cash rewards, because cash is a poor reward and does not make anyone content for long. **God said to Abraham, "I am . . . your exceedingly great reward"**

(Gen. 15:1). The Philippians had faith and works. Their faith worked in gifts and help to Paul in prison. Jesus stated this principle in Matthew 10:40, 42: "He who receives you receives me. . . . If anyone gives even a cup of cold water . . . because he is my disciple . . . he will certainly not lose his reward" (NIV). For one thing, they receive Christ, the unspeakable gift. God rewards the one who gives to any worker of His the same as the worker, the missionary supporter the same as the missionary, the one who prays as well as the one for whom he prays. So Paul could say to the Philippians who had provided for him in prison, "God shall supply all your need according to His riches in glory by Christ Jesus" (Phil. 4:19).

> God said to Abraham, "I am . . . your exceedingly great reward."

The people of faith in Scripture, like Abraham, had the will of God for their first priority and their second, and third, and so on. That meant seeking righteousness, seeking the lost sheep, giving their lives, and serving God with a single eye to His glory.

Faith in God and the profit motive are incompatible. In the second to last chapter of the Old Testament, Malachi is concerned with faith and affluence and confronts the people of Judah with their complaint that "it is futile to serve God. What did we gain?" (Mal. 3:14 NIV). God said this was a "harsh" thing to say (Mal. 3:13 NIV). But He heard when those who lived on a different level and feared the Lord, talked with one another: "'They will be mine,' says the LORD Almighty, 'in the day when I make up my treasured possession'" (Mal. 3:17 NIV). It was written in the "scroll of remembrance" (Mal. 3:16 NIV).

The Bible principle comes to us in ten words: "Not slothful in business; fervent in spirit; serving the Lord" (Rom. 12:11 KJV). "Fervent in spirit" (Greek, *zeontes*—"boiling"), refers not merely to red-hot revival meetings, but to doing business and earning a living, always as a service to God.

One famous English churchman in the days of King Henry VIII, Cardinal Wolsey, died charged with high treason. His famous words at the last were, "Had I but served my God as diligently as I have served the King, He would not have given me over in my gray hairs." The truth was that he had served the king only to serve himself. He made himself extremely wealthy and powerful. He would have been poorer if he had served God—but infinitely happier.

The people God can trust with prosperity are those who have not set their heart upon it, but upon Him. Jesus sat on the shore of the Sea of Galilee with the disciples and a huge catch of large fish in the boat. He Himself had told them to let down their nets for that haul. They had gone back to fishing and loved it. Jesus pointed to the boats and nets and the catch of fish. Then came the test. Jesus asked, "Do you love Me more than these?" (John 21:15). It was the same test as the Lord put before Abraham. Did he love God more than Isaac, the apple of his eye?

> The people God can trust with prosperity are those who have not set their heart upon it, but upon Him.

Much is said about wealth, prosperity, and poverty in Scripture. God doesn't want anybody to be poor. Godliness tends to wealth. Sin not only breeds poverty but also brings about the unholy accumulation of wealth to the damnation of those who possess it. James says to those who exploited and underpaid their workers, "Now listen, you rich people, weep and wail because of the misery that is coming upon you" (James 5:1 NIV).

The story of Abraham and Lot illustrates a complex subject. What I have written here are also Bible principles of faith, as I know them throughout Scripture. Each of us should apply them in our own sphere, whether as wealth creators or as dependent and needy, as we seek to live by faith in Christ.

chapter 9

Faith and the Names of God

The life-germ or life-spark in the Word is the name of the Lord. His name is the resurrection element of the Word of God, making the Bible "living and powerful" (Heb. 4:12). **The Bible is the resurrection book.** Scripture is balanced on His name.

There are, of course, many divine names mentioned in the Bible, and they are powerful, mighty, and rock solid. Each one highlights some aspect of the divine character. To know them brings understanding and faith. They are like power points where we can plug into what God is. We talk of people being promising because we see they have what it takes to accomplish a particular task. That is God. His names are promises. They show what is in Him, which brings us hope about what we can expect of Him.

An evangelist colleague, whom we'll call George, slipped into a church once and sat in the back. The leader said, "We will ask George to offer prayer." The evangelist didn't react, thinking it was some other George known in the church, since

| The Bible is the resurrection book. |

he heard his first name used so familiarly. It was, in fact, he whom the pastor was calling. "George" did not distinguish himself from others named George.

What's in a Name?

A thousand years ago, individuals in Europe had only one name. When more people were born they had to have a distinct designation, so they used their trade as a surname, John (the) Smith, John (the) Baker, John (the) Cook, John (the) Miller, and so on. Sometimes they used their father's personal name, such as John-son, James-son. Bible people did the same—James the son of Zebedee; Bar-abbas, "son of a father," probably illegitimate. There were many Jameses and Johns, so Jesus nicknamed them the "Sons of Thunder" (Mark 3:17). When Jesus met Simon, Andrew's brother, He said, "'You are Simon the son of Jonah. You shall be called Cephas,' (which is translated, A Stone)" (John 1:42). It is as "Peter" (the Rock) that we know Simon, the chief apostle.

We may think everyone knows who God is and that He doesn't need any name. "God" is not a personal name, but a common noun for a whole class, but God belongs to no class. Many people, however, believe in different deities or have confused ideas about God. His names tell us what kind of God He is and what people have found Him to be.

First Corinthians 8 has an important message about this as it explores the principles of liberty and our weaker brothers:

> For even if there are so-called gods, whether in heaven or on earth (as there are many gods and many lords), yet for us there is only one God, the Father, of whom are all things, and we for Him; and one Lord Jesus Christ, through whom are all things, and through whom we live. However, there is not in everyone that knowledge; for some, with consciousness of the idol, until now eat it as a thing offered to an idol; and their conscience, being weak, is defiled. (vv. 5–7)

He is the One who made all things, the Triune God of Christian revelation—Father, Son, and Spirit.

From our angle, God's divine names multiply once we think of Him. He is more than any single god is or goddess ever was, or all of them put together.

Actually He gave Himself various names. The great name of God was always "Yahweh" or "Lord" in the Old Testament. "Yahweh" disguised the mystery of God, which is revealed, through Christ, in the New Testament.

Each title describes something perceived about Him. When we look at an object, no two viewers have exactly the same impression. That is also true when we look at God.

He is the One who made all things.

Everyone has a different angle. Individuals each appreciate God differently. People have favorite titles for Him. For example, Nathaniel's spontaneous cry on meeting Jesus was, "Rabbi [i.e., Master], You are the Son of God! You are the King of Israel!" (John 1:49).

When Mary Magdalene saw Christ alive from the dead, her true regard for Him simply burst out: "Rabboni; which is to say, Master" (John 20:16 KJV).

Knowledge Is Devotion

True knowledge of the Lord transmutes into devotion and worship. George Herbert, the humble but aristocratic clergyman and famous poet, a favorite of King James I, loved the Lord dearly. He was often quoted by Charles Spurgeon for his line "How sweetly doth 'My Master' sound!"

What God is called lights up various aspects of deity that bear directly on faith. The favorite name in the book of Revelation is "the Lamb," used twenty-nine times. Faith in Christ as the Lamb is saving faith.

The first chapter of John's Gospel has twelve different titles for God: "the Word, the Light, the One and Only, Jesus Christ, the Lamb of God, the Son of God, the Messiah, Jesus of Nazareth, the son of Joseph, Rabbi, the King of Israel, the Son of Man."

He is also indicated by name phrases: "the one Moses wrote about in the Law" (John 1:45 NIV); "He will baptize you with the Holy Spirit" (Matt. 3:11b); "He who comes after me" (John 1:15); "the man on whom you see the Spirit come down" (John 1:33 NIV).

That last phrase, "the man on whom you see the Spirit come down," was a sign only for John the Baptist. But there was more. Christ is the One who would baptize in the Holy Spirit. That's who He is, not for a Bible character only, but for everyone. If we want to place the highest sign of all, it is that "He baptizes in the Spirit." That is who to look for and what to look for as pragmatic proof.

He wasn't styled by excessively ingratiating or grandiose words. He is pointed out by what He actually does. He baptizes in the Spirit. Not believing in that experience today, many throw away one of the greatest biblical evidences of the deity of our Lord and Savior Jesus Christ. This is needed as a personal experience, not just an agreement with it as theology.

In the Holy Spirit

The baptism in the Spirit is not trivial, common, or incidental. It is not a mere religious gesture—a hand waved to bless us. It is unmatched. It is the exclusive promise of Jesus Christ, and He alone has bestowed it. It is wonderful and hard evidence.

This experience is a finger pointing unmistakably and directly at the One with whom we are dealing. It settles questions. A down-to-earth character like "Doubting" Thomas, after he was baptized in the Spirit, needed no further convincing. Jesus, is the "Baptizer in the Spirit!" That is one of His most wonderful titles. It shows Him to be the true "I even I," the One and Only God, the same one who inspired the prophets and spoke through the lips of Joel, saying, "I will pour out My Spirit on all flesh" (Joel 2:28). He said He would, and He did. That's who He is.

Among the many titles of the Lord is "the Amen," first in Isaiah 65:16, "the God of truth" and last in Revelation 3:14, "the Amen." It is not just a formal ending to a prayer, a kind of "over and out." "Amen" actually never ends any prayers in the New Testament. Nor is it the same as, "Hear! Hear!" It declares a determined purpose to be behind whatever is said, as for example in someone's prayer. God is all that. "Whoever invokes a blessing in the land will do so by the God of [Amen]; he who takes an oath in the land will swear by the God of [Amen]" (Isa. 65:16 NIV). "These things says the Amen, the Faithful and True Witness" (Rev. 3:14).

God is the "Amen." He is "faithful and true" to what He said about Himself. He has a name or reputation for unchanging goodness. David prayed in 2 Samuel 7:23, saying that God went out to redeem a people, "to make a name for himself, and to perform great and awesome wonders" (NIV). David then invoked the Lord's personal faithfulness: "Now, LORD God. . . . Do as you promised, so that your name will be great forever" (2 Sam. 7:25–26 NIV). God would not fail Himself and lose His name and reputation.

This appears again many years later. "You are the LORD God, who chose Abram. . . . You sent miraculous signs and wonders. . . . You made a name for yourself, which remains to this day" (Neh. 9:7, 10 NIV). He will be faithful to what He taught us about Himself. Nehemiah knew the God Moses knew, the same unchanged character. We today know the God that the Bible people knew—a faithful covenant-keeping God.

God is the "Amen."

Ezekiel 20:9 reads, "For the sake of my name I did what would keep it from being profaned in the eyes of the nations they lived among and in whose sight I had revealed myself to the Israelites by bringing them out of Egypt" (NIV). What He did create was His fame, and He never lets Himself down.

We often pray, "Lord, glorify Thy holy name." We want everyone to honor and praise Him, but it actually means "confirm Your name," prove what You are. In His prayer recorded in John 17, Jesus said, "I have glorified You on the earth. I have finished the work which You have given me to do" (v. 4).

Christ Jesus had done what He said, and so God had been faithful to His purposes and promises. The name of God crystallizes His reputation. When we read of the name of the Lord in the Old Testament, it is always Yahweh, and Yahweh was always true to what He said and was. "He cannot deny Himself" (2 Tim. 2:13).

God's Support

God, being the God of Amen, has an attitude that is supportive, never indifferent. When we come to Him, He smiles upon us, responds in love, and says, "Amen." The word *Amen* means "faithful," "sure," "trustworthy." God tries to assure us and quiet our nervousness or misgivings by being the "Amen" God. He is dependable, not fickle and not changeable.

If the Lord had changed from how the Bible depicts Him, the Bible would be useless. We would not know what He is, but only as the ex-God of the Jews. However, Christians know He is the faithful and true God of the Bible.

The Omnipotent Yahweh

There are several "Yahweh" titles for God—each one given by revelation. Moses knew the name Yahweh, but not its depth of awesome wonder. Abraham also knew of Yahweh.

In Genesis 27:20, Jacob said, "The LORD [Yahweh] your God [Elohim] gave me success" (NIV). Once Jacob asked His name (Gen. 32:29) but got no reply. It was Yahweh, as Jacob very well knew, but Jacob wanted to know its significance. It was the same when Moses also asked His name and got the cryptic answer, "I AM WHO I AM" (Ex. 3:14). It meant that whatever He was, it was a secret. But it also meant it was a secret that would be opened and shared with those who believed, as time went on.

In one circumstance after another, people saw more and more what God was. His great name "Yahweh" was opened up, and new revelations were summed up with a second name. Each new Yahweh title gave us increased grounds for faith and for ever-increasing faith.

We have been given the privilege of knowing His name, not only of "calling on the name of the Lord," but we are called by His name (Isa. 43:7). His people are surnamed after Him, "the Lord's people," just as Israel was "Yahweh's people." Before Moses knew His name, the Lord said, "Do not draw near this place" (Ex. 3:5), but in the name of Jesus we do "draw near to God" (Heb. 7:19).

The Power of Authority

Jesus showed us what this great privilege is. It is a kind of power or authority. It is not a magic formula, but if we know what anyone is like, their strengths or weaknesses, we know how to handle them.

In Bible times people felt they gave themselves away when they gave their name away. It gave others an advantage over them. To ask their name was to ask about their character. When we come to God, we can come believing when we know His name. "Yahweh" was just a distinguishing title at the beginning, until by His deeds it was better understood.

Though identifying and exploring all of the "Yahweh" titles would necessitate another book, their richness must not be glossed over, for the names are doorways into God's very nature. Some of the most impacting names include:

Yahweh-Sabaoth—"The LORD of hosts," 1 Samuel 17:45. This appears more than 250 times in Scripture. We first hear it when David came against the Philistine warrior champion, Goliath, in that historic confrontation. David did not act upon what everyone else believed but did act upon the fact that God was with the army of Israel—the God of their "host." *Host* was the word for army in those times. It was realized that Israel's armies were not God's sole resource. He had other reserves, hosts upon hosts, and He was the God of Hosts.

He is on the side of all that love and trust Him. "If God is for us, who can be against us?" (Rom. 8:31). People of faith are in conflict with the whole philosophy of this world, in its aims and methods. But it is not a losing battle. **Christ has already overcome the world, and we are more than overcomers in Him.**

Yahweh-Jirah—"The-LORD-Will-Provide," Genesis 22:14. Abraham gave this name to the place where he went to offer Isaac, his only son. God stopped this human sacrifice, quite acceptable to people's ways and customs then, and gave Abraham a ram instead. This partly fulfilled Abraham's prophecy that God would provide a lamb, but the real fulfillment came later when God provided

> Christ has already overcome the world, and we are more than overcomers in Him.

the Lamb for the sins of the whole world. Greater than all He provides, material or spiritual, the supreme fulfillment of Yahweh-Jirah is Christ, who took our place in judgment. The world lives by God's material and physical supply but brushes past the very thing that is meant by God's providing.

Yahweh-Rophi—"The LORD who heals you," Exodus 15:26. This was a revelation about God, and God cannot be anything but what He is, whether to Israel or any other nation. Here, He was speaking of physical recovery, but God is a healing God in all situations where there is brokenness and illness—physically, domestically, nationally, spiritually. He is the Yahweh of salvation.

Yahweh-Nissi—"The-LORD-Is-My-Banner," Exodus 17:15. Moses gave this name to an altar of thanks to God after Israel had successfully thrown back a treacherous attack by the Amalekites at a time when Israel was little prepared for battle. Moses had prayed this victory through. God is the God of victory. As the world's most famous Christian hymn says, "I triumph still if thou abide with me."

Yahweh-Shalom—"The-LORD-Is-Peace," Judges 6:24. This was the name of another altar that was built by Gideon after the divine visitation to him to defend Israel from the Midianite invaders. In those prehistoric times, the world existed in a constant turmoil of war. The victory of Gideon began bloodlessly as the invaders panicked at Gideon's strategy of faith and demonstrated that God requires peace, not bloodshed. *Shalom* is the great Hebrew word so often used in Scripture. It spells out well-being, prosperity, good health, and safety. Jesus greeted His disciples with "Shalom!" He still does—He has "made peace through the blood of His cross" (Col. 1:20).

Yahweh-Tsidkenu—"THE LORD OUR RIGHTEOUS-NESS," Jeremiah 23:6. Jeremiah spoke of the One to come who would be a "Branch of righteousness; a King [to] reign and prosper, and [to] execute judgment and righteousness in the earth," and added "this is His name by which He will be called: THE LORD OUR RIGHTEOUSNESS" (23:5–6). This title firmly links Jesus Christ, the branch or shoot of David's dynasty, to Yahweh. It is God's own name, and it was realized in Christ who shed no blood but His own and brought in eternal righteousness.

Yahweh-Shammah—"THE LORD IS THERE," Ezekiel 48:35—the last words of the prophecy. It is a profound statement about God. He never arrives but is always "there." We cannot precede Him. Jesus said, "Where two or three are gathered together in My name, I am there" (Matt. 18:20). He is before all things, the eternal "I am" whenever and wherever we are, a "very present help." This is the mystery we can never fathom, but we can always enjoy.

Such Yahweh titles could be multiplied, for the Lord is all things to all men. The principle is, "According to your faith be it unto you." What God finally is, the last man on earth will not have discovered, but faith explores the great goodness of God.

Psalm 23, the Psalm of the Divine Shepherd, is an example. Behind each of its statements stands the mighty and wonderful name of Yahweh:

> The LORD is my shepherd; [Yahweh-Ra-ah]
> I shall not want. [Yahweh-Jireh]
> He makes me to lie down in green pastures;
> He leads me beside the still waters. [Yahweh-Shalom]

He restores my soul; [Yahweh-Rophi]
He leads me in the paths of righteousness
For His name's sake. [Yahweh-Tsidkenu]

Yea, though I walk through the valley of the shadow
of death,
I will fear no evil;
For You are with me; [Yahweh-Sabaoth]
Your rod and Your staff, they comfort me. [Yahweh-
Mekadesham]

You prepare a table before me in the presence of my
enemies; [Yahweh-Nissi]
You anoint my head with oil; [Yahweh-Rophi]
My cup runs over. [Yahweh-Jireh]
Surely goodness and mercy shall follow me
All the days of my life; [Yahweh-Shalom]
And I will dwell in the house of the LORD
Forever. [Yahweh-Shammah]

God said, "I am who I am." He **can't be anything other than what He is,** at any time, for anyone, in all dispensations and places and circumstances. The names we have mentioned are simply to commemorate moments and events when men and women proved what He is.

Scripture hammers home the fact that **we can trust God because of who He is.** It is His identity that is laid out in the Bible. Someone may tell us his or her experiences prove God, but the Scriptures must confirm it. Experience can come from other sources. First John 4:1–2 states, "Do not

> God can't be anything other than what He is.

believe every spirit. . . . Every spirit that confesses that Jesus Christ has come in the flesh is of God."

Simple Believing

Sometimes believing in God is described as "believing on the name of the Lord." John 2:23 says, "Many people saw the miraculous signs he was doing and believed in his name" (NIV). His name to them meant miracle signs. God has various names that sum up what He is.

> We can trust God because of who He is.

We believe what people say, or we may believe in them. We consider them as having integrity. But **whom we believe in is all-important.** We may believe in a doctor or a solicitor or a minister and trust this person for what he or she can do for us, such as putting ourselves into a surgeon's hands. But what about God? We are not dealing with someone of limited skills, but He is the all-sufficient One, with whom we can repose our entire confidence in all our affairs and give our lives over to Him. After all, Jesus Himself declared, "Trust in God; trust also in me" (John 14:1 NIV) and, "He who believes in Me, believes not in Me, but in Him who sent Me" (John 12:44).

Look again at those two verses, and you will note that "Me" occurs four times. This is a special thing in Scripture when it represents God as speaking. He keeps on using and stressing the pronouns "Me" or "I," "Myself." The book of Isaiah is the main example except in the words of Jesus.

> Whom we believe in is all-important.

The purpose is to encourage us to have confidence in Him because of His divine integrity. This "I" is emphasized in special ways. "I, even I, am the LORD, / And besides Me there is no savior"; "There is no other Rock; / I know not one." From this, a warning arises: "Woe to him who strives with his Maker!" (Isa. 43:11; 44:8; 45:9). If we cannot trust God who made us, then we are lost.

The Holy One of Israel

When the Bible was written, everyone followed their gods, except many Israelite people who had nothing to do with the visible idols. They called upon the invisible God and knew something of Him. From them came the first streaks of civilized freedom, one thousand years before Greece or Rome existed. We can't be better than what we believe. Civilization in every age rests upon the revelation of a God of integrity to whom we are all accountable.

Israel knew they could not treat the Lord as just another one in the pantheon of deities. He was transcendent, "the Holy One of Israel," far above everything else that existed. King Solomon dedicated a temple to God but said, "Will God really dwell on earth? The heavens, even the highest heaven, cannot contain you. How much less this temple I have built!" (1 Kings 8:27 NIV).

No one ever trusted the pagan gods. No one committed his or her life to Aphrodite or Zeus. It is hard for modern people to appreciate what civilization at that time was like. With all their temples, altars, practices, and celebration of pagan festivals, people had no religious feeling, no spiritual ideals whatsoever. Pagans busily attended to their altars because they feared the gods' turning nasty. But the *real* God above all other gods calms us, nurtures us, and brings us to Him, securely.

The Lord (Yahweh) permeates the whole of life. "Besides Me . . . there is no other" says God in Isaiah 45:6. He is separate and holy. On one occasion Moses prayed and God gave Him new light and understanding. It is described in the book of Exodus, chapter 34. This is a very important passage for everyone and to all the nations on earth, whether they admit it or not:

> The LORD descended in the cloud and stood with him there, and proclaimed the name of the LORD. And the LORD passed before him and proclaimed, "The LORD, the LORD God, merciful and gracious, longsuffering, and abounding in goodness and truth, keeping mercy for thousands, forgiving iniquity and transgression and sin, by no means clearing the guilty, visiting the iniquity of the fathers upon the children and the children's children to the third and the fourth generation." So Moses made haste and bowed his head toward the earth, and worshiped. Then he said, "If now I have found grace in Your sight, O Lord, let my Lord, I pray, go among us, even though we are a stiff-necked people; and pardon our iniquity and our sin, and take us as Your inheritance." (vv. 5–9)

The Lord came down in the cloud and stood there with him and proclaimed His name, the Lord. And he passed in front of Moses, proclaiming the Lord, the Lord, the compassionate and gracious God, slow to anger, abounding in love and faithfulness, maintaining love to thousands, and forgiving wickedness, rebellion, and sin. Yet **He does not leave the guilty unpunished.**

This passage links God's name "the Lord" to His nature, gracious, loving, and long-suffering. William Barclay tells us that *long-suffering* is a Christian word. It does not occur in classical Greek at all and very seldom in later Greek. To Greeks, long-suffering was not a virtue, but an unmanly weakness. Dr. Barclay said,

> He does not leave the guilty unpunished.

"The great Greek virtue was the refusal to tolerate any insult or injury, vengeance." It was Israel only who saw the spirit of forgiveness and long-suffering as a virtue. There is more true morality in Exodus 34 than all Homer or Aeschylus ever wrote.

The Lord says, "I," over and over. When men or women talk about themselves and it is all "I," "I," they are vain, egotists, and narcissists. No one alive is that special, but God says, "There is none beside Me" and constantly uses this word I when addressing us. He is a firm foundation.

But the Lord does more than say "I." He lays extra emphasis upon it in various ways. Many times He says, "I, the Lord." There are double repetitions, "I, even I," or "I myself," or "I am He, I am He" (Isa. 43:11, 25; 41:14; 46:4 NIV). This has the purpose of explaining what and who He is. He often links it with a further statement about Himself. For example, "I am the LORD, your God, / The Holy One of Israel, your Savior; / I gave Egypt for your ransom, / Ethiopia and Seba in your place" (Isa. 43:3).

That is the kind of thing He says. He is unique and wants to encourage us to trust Him for what He can do. "Thus says the LORD, your Redeemer" (Isa. 43:14). "I, even I, am He who blots out your transgressions for My own sake" (Isa. 43:25). No one else was like Him or did such things. If we don't trust Him, there's no one else. "There is no other name . . . among men by which we must be saved" (Acts 4:12). It was a common fact. No one knew anyone else who could save, except God. Psalm 73:25–28 says:

> Whom have I in heaven but You?
> And there is none upon earth that I desire besides You.
> My flesh and my heart fail;
> **But God is the strength of my heart and my portion**
>   **forever.**
> For indeed, those who are far from You shall perish;
> You have destroyed all those who desert You for
>   harlotry.
> But it is good for me to draw near to God;
> I have put my trust in the Lord GOD,
> That I may declare all Your works.

In our lives, there is no one else to be the One except God Himself.

Now we come to something unusual. First, remember this about God, that we "know in part," not "face to face" (1 Cor. 13:12). We know, but we don't know it all. Haldane the scientist said, "Creation is not only more wonderful than we think, but more wonderful than we can think."

> "But God is the strength of my heart and my portion forever."

A strange expression is used in Isaiah 41:4, "I, the LORD, . . . I am He." The verb "am" is not in the original

Hebrew. It is put in by the translators, but actually God is speaking of Himself as "I-He."

It is an example of the greatness and wonder of the Lord and His name. When Manoah asked the angel of the Lord His name, the Lord said, "Why do you ask my name? It is beyond understanding" (Judg. 13:18 NIV). The same word is used in Isaiah 9:6; "His name will be called / Wonderful." His name is a wonder, a mystery. The word is used to describe Christ's miracles in Matthew 21:15, "The chief priests and scribes saw the wonderful things that He did." God's name is a wonder name, a miracle name. It holds secrets about Him.

What does "I-He" mean, or what does it tell us? We can find something more about it from two other passages of Scripture: Deuteronomy 32:39, "See now that I myself am He! / There is no god besides me" (NIV); and Zechariah 12:10, "I will pour on the house of David and on the inhabitants of Jerusalem the Spirit of grace and supplication; then they will look on Me whom they have pierced; Yes, they will mourn for Him as one mourns for his only son." So, "Me" is the same One as "Him" whom they pierced and for whom they are mourning, the same God speaking. It is the wonder-mystery of the Godhead.

The words *Me* and *Him* are also described as a child of Israel, like an only child. Isaiah said, "Unto us a Child is born, / Unto us a Son is given" (Isa. 9:6). Zechariah spoke about this child as being pierced. Matthew's Gospel in the first verse identifies this "Child" and "Son," saying, "Jesus Christ, the Son of David, the Son of Abraham," and Jesus called Himself "the Son of Man." Now both Abraham and David had special sons, but they were not the true, promised Son that the prophecy in Isaiah said would come. The true Son of the house of David was Jesus, the Christ.

This is the Son, "the only child" whom God spoke about through Zechariah, saying: "They will look on Me whom they have pierced. . . . they will mourn for Him . . . and grieve for Him" (Zech. 12:10). So the Me is the Him, and the I is the He. Jesus said, "I and My Father [I and He] are one" (John 10:30).

Since God is "I am," His Son also is "I am." The Father is "I" and the Son is "He." The One who was pierced was both "Me" and "Him." The Father was involved with the Son at Calvary, and we read "God was in Christ reconciling the world to Himself" (2 Cor. 5:19). God called Himself "your Redeemer" in the Old Testament, and in the New Testament the precious blood of Jesus Christ, who was pierced for us, redeems us. That piercing of the Son pierced the heart of the Father.

Isaiah 45:6 also uses the great title of God, "I am," "I am the LORD, and there is no other." It was given to Moses as, "I AM WHO I AM" (Ex. 3:14). The Hebrew experts have translated this various ways, but it is not possible to put it into other languages or even to make good grammar out of it in Hebrew.

Moses asked God about His name. He already knew that He was the Lord (Hebrew, *Yahweh*). Abraham also knew this name, but its significance was not yet revealed. The experience he had of God was as "God Almighty" (*El Shaddai*), which is only one side of divine greatness. He promised Sarah a son and she laughed, but the Lord said, "Is anything too hard for the LORD?" (Gen. 18:14). It needed a display of something more than omnipotence. Moses saw it, and then the meanings of the name "Lord," which were veiled, began to emerge.

Later of course the whole process of revelation was changed. It was no longer through prophets but by His Son, Jesus the Christ (Heb. 1:1–2).

The "I am" title of God is applied to Jesus in John's Gospel. In some instances Christ's word "I am" is exactly the same as the "I am" of the Lord in the Old Testament Scriptures. Jesus said in John 10:11, "I am the good shepherd," but Psalm 23:1 says, "The LORD is my shepherd," and Psalm 80:1 refers to the Lord as the "Shepherd of Israel." Jesus said, "I am the bread of life" (John 6:35), and in Deuteronomy 8:3, the words of God are bread.

> God can't be put in a picture or carved in marble or put into words.

He used "I am" also in the absolute sense in John 8:58. "Before Abraham was, I AM," He stated. He did not say, "Before Abraham was, I was," but "I AM." Christ spoke similarly to God, as when God spoke to Moses, "This is what you are to say to the Israelites: I AM has sent me to you" (3:14 NIV). He is the timeless One to whom past and future are alike.

God can't be put in a picture or carved in marble or put into words. God forbade the Israelites to make an image of Him because it would convey a wrong idea. Some idols are so horrible that such portraits would please no self-respecting god.

The heathen wanted something to see and feel. They made images out of wood or clay. But Zephaniah 3:17 shows something the heathen didn't know about—that the Lord is "mighty to save" (NIV). This mighty God was not mere material or flesh. He was of infinitely more wonderful substance, too real for our weak eyes. God is a Spirit. He said, "Truly You are God, who hide Yourself, / O God of Israel, the Savior!" (Isa. 45:15).

God said, "I AM WHO I AM," and we shall gain much insight as time goes by. Moses learned

The Spirit of God guides us into all truth.

what God was when he appeared before Pharaoh and even more when he entered the tabernacle. "He made known His ways to Moses," the psalmist wrote, "His acts to the children of Israel" (Ps. 103:7).

The Spirit of God guides us into all truth. We cannot grasp the ocean of God in our span and know all things at once. We shall learn as He fulfills the Word.

Today we talk about the information overload. The Internet and other sources supply more detail and facts than we have time to use or absorb. Businesspeople find that it is impossible to go through all the masses of information at their disposal before they make a decision.

But neither can believers know everything about God, only that we can trust Him. **True knowledge of God galvanizes, burns in our hearts, and moves us.** Jesus said, "Learn of me" (Matt. 11:29 KJV), that is, about Him from Him. To know Him is life itself.

True knowledge of God galvanizes, burns in our hearts, and moves us.

chapter 10

Faith for the Night

John's Gospel is the subtlest in the Bible. It is full of literal events and expressions, which we are meant to read in an understanding way. As John said, "These are written that you may believe . . . and that believing you may have life" (John 20:31).

The Greeks came and said to Philip, "Sir, we would like to see Jesus." They were in darkness. The Greeks were then the most educated race on earth, but spiritually benighted. This is what one writer says about their times and their religious ideas: they were "aware of a supernatural reality [but they did not] credit this reality with benevolence towards mankind, [being] blind, often destructive in their operation."

The Greeks knew of no Father in heaven giving His Son out of love for mankind. Jesus spoke to them of giving His life for them. Their own ideas were of dangerous gods. For example, one of their pagan plays concerned the god Dionysus, who became angry with the king of Thebes, Pentheus, because the king had not honored him. The god makes the king and his mother insane, and she tore her son limb from limb. Paul the apostle was well acquainted with such stories and called those days, "times of ignorance."

"It Is I; Do Not Be Afraid"

Now, look at the well-known story in John 6. The disciples, rowing hard against wind and current in the darkness, suddenly see a phantom figure gliding across the churning surface of the lake. Their fears doubled. Hardy men as they were, they shouted with terror. Then above the howl of the winds, cutting across the spume came Christ's voice, "It is I; do not be afraid" (6:20). **Jesus was a carpenter or builder, not a seaman, but they knew that with Christ in the vessel they could smile at the storm. He was the conqueror of devils and darkness.**

> Jesus was the conqueror of devils and darkness.

That is what the multitude noticed. Jesus had such a tremendous stature in their eyes that when the disciples went without Him, they were "alone." A dozen weather-hardened fishermen together, boatmen, experts on familiar waters, but because Jesus was not with them they were "alone"! They were worse than alone. They were lonely and in the dark.

If all the six billion people on this planet had no Jesus, we would all be alone together, in the darkness. This world would be as dreadful and lonely as winter in the ice-clad Antarctic. But He's here. We are not alone in an unfriendly universe. We have a Friend who promises to take care of us forever. "Let not your heart be troubled; you believe in God, believe also in Me," Jesus said in John, chapter 14. "In My Father's house

> If all the six billion people on this planet had no Jesus, we would all be alone together, in the darkness.

are many mansions; if it were not so, I would have told you. I go to prepare a place for you. And if I go and prepare a place for you, I will come again and receive you to Myself; that where I am, there you may be also. And where I go you know, and the way you know" (vv. 1–4).

And in the book of Matthew, chapter 28, Jesus told us what to do, then comforted us: "All authority has been given to Me in heaven and on earth," He said. "Go therefore and make disciples of all the nations, baptizing them in the name of the Father and of the Son and of the Holy Spirit, teaching them to observe all things that I have commanded you; and lo, I am with you always, even to the end of the age" (vv. 18–20).

Even in a waterlogged old tub clutched by hissing waves, the disciples were immediately relieved when Jesus said, "It is I, do not be afraid." The words recorded in the Greek (*ego eimi*) are literally "I am." **Because *He is*, we can feel safe.** "Yea, though I walk through the valley of the shadow of death, / I will fear no evil; / For You are with me" (Ps. 23:4). That is all we need to know.

The Gospel of John, though, adds the final touch (6:21): "Then they willingly received Him into the boat, and immediately the boat was at the land where they were going." No doubt they were

> Because He is, we can feel safe.

more than willing to take Him into the boat, but Mark 6:48 says He "would have passed them by." It was up to them. If they were willing, He would be with them. That's the way of Jesus always. He waits for the invitation.

Now the important result was that *immediately* they reached the shore where they were heading. When Jesus arrived, they arrived! **When Jesus comes to us, we have arrived.** That is life's highest point and the ultimate goal. Christ is the shore for which we are heading. He's the purpose of all our travels.

There's an interesting confrontation with Jesus in Matthew 8:19–20. A man told Jesus, "I will follow You wherever You go." He thought Jesus was going somewhere and that if he went with Him he would get somewhere too. He wanted a place in life, especially with a man who talked about a kingdom. He was a social climber. What blindness! Jesus isn't going to be something or going to get somewhere. He *is* the Somewhere, the Everywhere, the Beginning and the Ending. The kingdom *is* Jesus.

> When Jesus comes to us, we have arrived.

The Light of the World

He's the only Light of the World. If you follow any light, where do you find yourself? At the light! Follow the light of Christ and you find yourself at His feet. He lights the way only in one direction—to Himself. He is the Way, both its beginning and its ending, "the land where they were going."

There are those who invite us to join them in their search for truth and for light. **But if they don't have light already how can they find anything?** They could fall over the truth and not know what it was. They say, "It is better to travel hopefully than to arrive." In other words, search forever and never find.

But Jesus said, "Search and you shall find." Searching is all some men know, always looking for something, but they don't know what it is or what it looks like or even if it is there! Paul warned Timothy about such blind guides who are "always learning and never able to come to the knowledge of the truth" (2 Tim. 3:7).

That is why they don't like Christian believers, for we say that we have found it. Some of us don't want to be eternal wanderers, like the legend of the *Flying Dutchman,* the phantom ship said to be

> If they don't have light already how can they find anything?

seen under full sail in storms off the Cape of Good Hope, never able to enter harbor. With Christ we have already reached harbor. He is our eternal home out of the darkness.

When Jesus went into the Garden of Gethsemane, He led the disciples. They carried no torches or lanterns. He resorted so often to that grove of olive trees to pray that He knew every path. It was moonlit but dark under the trees. Without Him, they needed lanterns. John remembered Christ's words: "I am the light of the world. He who follows Me shall not walk in darkness, but have the light of life" (John 8:12).

Jesus makes lanterns redundant. The world makes its own artificial light, proudly independent. They prefer brainpower to God's power. Moses said, "If you do not obey the LORD your God and do not carefully follow all his commands and decrees. . . . the LORD will afflict you with . . . confusion of mind. At midday you will grope about like a blind man in the dark" (Deut. 28:15, 28–29 NIV).

Job saw it happening in his day and records in 12:24–25, "He deprives the leaders . . . of their reason. . . . They grope in darkness with no light" (NIV). And Isaiah 59:9–10 testifies, "We look for light, but there is darkness! . . . We grope for the wall like the blind . . . We stumble at noonday."

Paul told the Greeks at Corinth that the world through wisdom did not know God (1 Cor. 1:21). That is one verse in the Bible no one can contradict. Libraries are filled with the reasoning of the most perceptive brains that ever existed, and they tell us precisely nothing except that they are sure of nothing. They are but earthly lanterns and torches!

The most confused people on earth are those relying on reason alone. They don't know how to spell out the truth. Faith clarifies the mind. The odd thing is, it doesn't stop at faith. It becomes knowledge and light. Faith pulls the blinds up, not down.

A Different Kind of Darkness

We've had two-and-a-half thousand years of thought, and today it is exactly what Moses, Job, and Isaiah said—men grope like the blind with their hands on the wall at noonday. Since Christ came, it has been a glorious noon. "Your light has come!" (Isa. 60:1); "The Sun of Righteousness shall arise" (Mal. 4:2); "Its truth is seen in him . . . and the true light is already shining" (1 John 2:8 NIV). Jesus said, "If you would believe you would see the glory of God" (John 11:40). **But the glory of God is here for all to see.**

> The glory of God is here for all to see.

Now, John talked about another kind of darkness in chapter 20, verse 1, saying that early on the first day of the week, while it was still dark, Mary Magdalene went to the tomb.

Once again John had a double meaning behind his words "while it was still dark." When Christ rose the dawn came for the whole world. But for those dreadful hours, so far as the whole world was concerned, and the disciples, and Mary Magdalene in particular, it didn't just seem dark, it was very dark.

When Christ died, the candle of hope was snuffed out. For those three days and nights, truth was eclipsed. Jesus warned the disciples this time would come, as in John 9:4–5, "The night is coming when no one can work. As long as I am in the world, I am the light of the world." He had gone—they thought. The night had come. "It was still dark," but not for long!

Mary "came running" to Peter and John, and immediately they jumped up and both of them started out for the tomb and "both were running." Mary also found her way back. John was apparently younger and got to the tomb first and stood outside, bending over to look inside. The opening was not a six-foot doorway but only half that size. John deemed it important to record that he saw "the strips of linen lying there" (John 20:5 NIV). Peter then rushed up. Being the impetuous mortal, he went into the tomb. Then again John mentioned that Peter saw the strips of linen.

Then John distinguished the way these three people saw, but used three different words. There are also three different kinds of people represented with Mary, Peter, and John, who saw in different ways.

When Mary saw the stone was removed, the word *saw* is the ordinary word meaning "to see" (Greek, *blepo*). When

John came he stooped down and saw in the same way as Mary—he simply saw the linen wrappings along with everything else. It was a casual look, incidental.

That is one way of seeing. Many hear testimonies of Christ, His transforming power, His miracle healings, or even pick up the Bible and read, but it is all casual. They hardly give such things a second thought. There's no faith in that kind of seeing. In fact, it is blind seeing, a dark lantern and physical only, the spiritual totally missed. At that point for Mary, it was "still dark," and it is for all who shrug their shoulders at the supernatural evidences of the living Jesus.

Peter now came and, to begin with, he went into the tomb. There, "he beheld" the linen wrappings, a different word (Greek, *theoreo*). That is, he paid particular attention to them. Whatever had happened to the body of Jesus, those linen wrappings should not be there. They should have gone with Him. It was strange. It needed an explanation. But he left it at that.

That is the second way of seeing. People take notice and want an explanation. The universe is wonderful. Strange things happen. Prayers are answered. Dying people recover. Nature is incredible. Such things leave many guessing, even the scientists. Millions admit there's a mystery, something unusual. But it remains a mystery, awaiting an answer. They even enjoy the mystery and perceive nothing in the gloom of the tomb.

Then John went into the tomb. He saw what Peter had "beheld," but John had the eyes of a seer. It says, "he saw and believed" (John 20:8). The Gospel distinguishes this with a different word (Greek, *eiden,* from *horao*). Verse 9 says, "As yet they did not know the Scripture, that He must rise again from the dead." In that case, we don't know precisely when

John started believing. But we know one thing for sure—he believed in Christ, that is, he believed Jesus was always the Master, always the winner. John didn't know and could not imagine anything so fantastic as resurrection, but his faith rested when he didn't understand. Somehow Jesus had won and tossed those grave clothes aside. John "perceived."

That is the third way of seeing; to "see and believe." We can look around, observe the same things as others, the same Bible, the same testimonies, the same world, but with different eyes, understanding deep within us. **Our spirit recognizes our origin**, and that "something" is personal, caring, and real.

> Our spirit recognizes our origin.

Faith Enables Sight

Mary continued seeing, yet not seeing. She saw two angels, and then saw Jesus, but it was still no more than gazing, like Peter inspecting the grave clothes (the *theoreo* word). Then Jesus spoke, and what her eyes didn't tell her, her ears did. Nobody could say, "Mary," like He did. "She turned herself" (John 20:16 KJV). It was the greatest change—a reversal. She recognized He was alive.

Faith does that and enables us to see He who is invisible. It is *He!* "We see Jesus!" He's the One. He's the Bible God, the Bible Jesus, the One who should be dead and isn't. What we see is what He was and keeps on being: winning human hearts, answering prayer, healing the sick, blessing our very soul, creating and re-creating. We "see and believe." Things are happening; there is evidence, and it fits only one Person, Jesus.

It is dark until Jesus comes. It is lonely until He comes. It is all mystery until He comes. And when we are willing to take Him into the boat, we arrive at the shore where we are heading. But sometimes, we are all immersed in a vast sea of unseen forces. Can you see radio waves or the magnetic fields by which the stars keep their ancient places? All around us, even going through our very bodies, are powerful emissions that we can detect only by instruments. Some radiation could destroy us before we ever detected it. Human perceptions are very limited. Even your cat can hear what you cannot.

The first words Jesus said to His disciples were, "Come and see" (John 1:39). He came to make us see and see in the dark. His concern was for things as vital to our lives as anything in nature. The great theme in John's Gospel is inner sight, seeing more than meets the eye. Spiritual reality belongs to a different order. Physical eyes can't discern the spiritual.

John mentioned that some witnessed Christ's miracles and made nothing of them. Sheep nourish a blind life within the brain, and people spiritually can be no better. The visible displays invisible—"The heavens declare the glory of God" (Ps. 19:1), but not to those without faith. Another thing is that, at present, the world lies in wickedness and spiritual darkness. The unseen is doubly unseen.

In the natural realm, we have ways to render the invisible visible. The infrared camera can take photographs on the blackest of nights. Police use radar helicopters and can find a thief in the dark, even under trees. In the spiritual realm, no one need walk in darkness. But there is a way to see Him who is invisible, and the instrument we need to do that with is faith. It is our infrared camera. We have eyes to see and can walk in the ignorance and blackness of our world with confidence, as in daylight. Believers are "children of the day" (1 Thess. 5:5 KJV), and "we walk by faith, not by sight" (2 Cor. 5:7).

Faith is like a lamp; it is of no use in daylight. The only chance faith will ever have is now, in a world of sin and trouble. It can't operate in heaven where there is nothing at risk. Faith will be lost in sight, and Scripture verifies this. Paul, in the book of 1 Corinthians, explained it: "For now we see in a mirror, dimly, but then face to face. Now I know in part, but then I shall know just as I also am known. And now abide faith, hope, love, these three; but the greatest of these is love" (13:12–13).

Faith is our autopilot for the flight, not for when we land and walk the crystal floor of glory. Faith is like gold. It can stand the fire. Faith that doesn't come through the fire is like "fool's gold," pyrite that only looks like the real thing. **Fairweather faith isn't faith at all.** Faith is not possible except in storm and cloud.

John's Gospel uses the word *darkness* fifteen times. Its course is set in 1:5: "The light shines in the darkness, but the darkness has not understood it" (NIV).

The word *understood* is worth a second glance. Other Bible versions use different words—*understood* is from the NIV. The KJV uses the word *comprehended.* The Interlinear translates it as *overtook,* in Weymouth as *overpowered,* and the NEB

> **Fairweather faith isn't faith at all.**

as *mastered.* The word John used has all those and other similar meanings—to grasp, obtain, overtake, surprise, apprehend, seize, or suddenly come upon.

Why did he use such expressions and ambiguous allusions? The reason is very important. He wants to test readers, not browbeat them or blind them with science. They can interpret his words as they choose and that way tie in with what he is saying. It will prove what they are.

Now look at that word again. It has that long list of meanings, telling us what the darkness cannot do, such as overcoming, mastering, and conquering. Use whatever word you like, but John was telling us that no matter what the threat of darkness, whether overtaking or seizing or surprising or anything else, there is no way by which the darkness can prevail against light.

On the Winning Side

Believers are on the winning side. They are not odds-on favorites; they are unconditional winners. Darkness never gets the better of light, and John demonstrated this in various ways. One way is that sometimes he mentioned physical darkness or earthly night and gave it a special significance— it was a hint for us to see between the lines.

Let's look first at John 3:1–7. This Scripture says, "A man of the Pharisees named Nicodemus, a member of the Jewish ruling council. . . . came to Jesus by night" (NIV). He was really a delegate from the leading religionists. What Jesus said to him is famous: "You must be born again." Incidentally, He meant not only Nicodemus but also the people who had sent him. He said, "anyone," and in verse 7 Jesus says "you" in the plural.

Now, the Gospel of John mentions Nicodemus three times and on each occasion reminds us that he came by night. John wanted us to catch what he was getting at, and it wasn't just that it was after sunset, but that Nicodemus came in the darkness of those times. Israel had lost the light. There was a religious power failure, and with all their brilliant rabbis not one could repair the fault.

Jerusalem had all the most elaborate, expensive, and ornamental religious equipment of the day. They had thousands of priests taking their turns; a temple that was a world wonder with a gold roof no bird could perch upon; impressive daily pageantry and sacrifices; wonderful male voice choirs; the finest hymnbook ever written (the Psalms); and especially, "the law, the prophets, and the writings"—the complete Old Testament, which is the Jewish Scriptures.

It was all there. It reminds me of the electric wiring set up to illuminate a city, with the lamps and chandeliers swinging in the dead darkness. Their Jerusalem Temple was a kind of illustration. It had no light and no windows. The priests moved around inside using oil lamps—a picture of artificial religion, "having a form of godliness but denying its power" (2 Tim. 3:5). Originally the Holy Place was illuminated by the glory of God, and no window was needed. But now the glory had departed.

Faith brings understanding.

These Bible teachers of Israel were all so sure that they were right. Jesus was sure that they were wrong. He said to Nicodemus, "You are Israel's teacher, and do you not understand these things?" (John 3:10 NIV). **Faith brings understanding.** It is a strange but real experience. Suddenly, when you trust Christ, the future is like day breaking on the horizon.

There is such a thing as false sight, though. There are mirages in which things only look real. In the desert, an oasis appears, but there is no water there. Many leaders at the time of Jesus had a mirage religion. They had a fierce belief, but it was as arid as the desert. They had no water. They defended their religion fiercely and were prepared to die for it. They did a lot for it, but it did nothing for them. It was law, but it was not light.

There are even believers in the Bible who thought of God as a has-been, used-to-be deity. The active God of the Bible is to them no longer active in the same way. If God doesn't do what He did, then how can we say He is the same?

We can't contend for the original gospel and then deny its original power. People can be converted to a doctrine instead of to an experience of life, born of the Spirit. Faith switches on the power, and then believers become "a city . . . set on a hill [that] cannot be hidden" (Matt. 5:14), full of light.

The Right Vision

That's common human psychology, seen especially in religion. People are so long in the gloom that they can't stand sunshine. They have warmed their fetters, wearing them so long that they want to keep them. Faith in Christ means freedom, not slavery and not gloom. But some fiercely resent such benefits. Their prison doors are open, but they shrink back into their cell. Men prefer darkness rather than light, it is true, but Christ brings freedom and all we have to do is what Christ told us to do—ask. "So I say to you, ask, and it will be given to you," Jesus promised. "Seek, and you will find; knock, and it will be opened to you. For everyone who asks receives, and he who seeks finds, and to him who knocks it will be opened" (Luke 11:9–10).

Vision is important for faith. And there are but three kinds of vision or seeing: with the eyes, with the rational mind, and by heart-faith. Of those three, heart-faith gets faith off the drawing board and into production. That is what John chapter 9 is all about. The words of Jesus Himself at the end of the chapter sum matters up: "For judgment I have come into this world, so that the blind will see and those who see will become blind. . . . If you were blind, you would not be guilty of sin; but now that you claim you can see, your guilt remains" (vv. 39, 41 NIV).

When Steven Langton divided the Bible into chapters seven hundred years ago, he started chapter 9 at the wrong place. It is the story of Christ healing the blind man when men in the temple took up stones to kill Jesus (8:59). It should read like this, "Jesus hid himself, slipping away from the temple grounds," *and* (9:1) "As he went along, he saw a man blind from birth" (NIV). Escaping from fanatics who were trying to murder Him, Jesus still could feel concern for an afflicted man suffering the lifelong calamity of sightlessness. That's the Jesus touch.

However, that is not how the disciples looked on him. They were used to seeing blind beggars, but took notice when Jesus did. He said nothing for a moment, so they, of course, felt compelled to make some comment. So they simply articulated the common platitudes as to why the man was born blind, the half-baked ideas of those times. It was either his sin before he was born or his parents' sin.

Jesus was no more interested in philosophizing about illness than a surgeon is with a patient on the operating table. He offered no explanations. "The reason the Son of God appeared was to destroy the devil's work" (1 John 3:8 NIV), He explained. His answer was not words, but "by His stripes we are healed" (Isa. 53:5). **God** speaks, but His words are creative. He says Amen to His own words and **does what He says.**

Jesus immediately solved the question of whether it was the man or his parents who sinned. He said, "Neither!" It astonished them. It upset two thousand years of religious ideas. But then, to heal a blind man was also an upset in the two-thousand-year reign of their own beliefs.

Jesus followed the question of healing and the man's sin by saying that this happened so that the work of God might be displayed in his life. He meant exactly that, the works of God. Hadn't God made man of clay at the beginning? Could the works of God with clay be repeated? If He could do that, it said a lot about who He was. Later He said, "You believe in God, believe also in Me" (John 14:1). He was giving us all reason to do so. He did what God did.

> God does what He says.

It never was the intent of God for people to be blind. Adam was not created blind. God wanted no one blind, by birth or at any other time. The work of God is sight, not sightlessness. He doesn't want us to go through life blind, spiritually or physically.

God did not make this man blind just to heal him. That is fatalism. We are not God's guinea pigs. God is not cynical. What Jesus really said was, "Let the works of God be done," not, "So that the works be done" (that is how this verse should be translated).

What Jesus did, though, was turn this marvelous wonder into an acted parable. He said that as long as it is day we *must* (imperative) do the work of Him who sent Christ. Night is coming when no man can work. While Jesus is in the world He is the Light of the World. Do you notice it? Jesus changes Me to We. *We* must do the work of the One who sent Christ. It is the same work, of course, for which He sent Christ—to bring light and sight. That's the business God is in, and we are His business partners, or maybe His shop assistants, handing out what He has for all who come. The One who said, "Let there be light," also said to His disciples in the Sermon on the Mount, "You are the light of the world" (Matt. 5:14).

We go to church and find comfort. That is the right thing to do, but it is not the greatest purpose. We are lights in the darkness for the storm-tossed. Moses entered God's presence not merely to enjoy it, but to bring some of the glory back with him for Israel to see. It was seen in his face.

One of the Seven Wonders of the World was the Pharos lighthouse at Alexandria, then the tallest building in the world and the only lighthouse. Its light was simply a fire. Pharos was also a religious symbol. Light in the darkness was a rare thing then. It was a rare thing spiritually. At first there was only Christ, until He lit fire in His disciples and sent them to "scatter fire on the earth" so the storm-tossed could find their way home. There's still no other light.

Why, though, would Jesus give this man sight? No one asked Him, no one pressured Him, and the man himself didn't call upon Him as blind Bartimaeus did. We know Christ had the right to heal, and He had the power, but why bother?

Theologians call it a sovereign act of God, but that explains nothing. *Sovereign* means the same thing as God acting as He pleased. He always does anyway. Why did God choose to act that way? What motivated Him?

It just isn't good enough to talk about sovereignty. Jesus didn't come to tell us God was mysterious and beyond all understanding. **In His coming, He assured us of His unfailing goodness.** It was more than knowing Him. It was understanding Him. He was not a God of uncertain character who might at any time manifest inexplicable bursts of kindness, without rhyme or reason.

Jesus performed wonders to explain God, who is unchangeable, and to create in us confidence, as the psalmist said, "I will not take my love from him, nor will I ever betray my faithfulness" (Ps. 89:33 NIV). Without God's solid reliability, faith is impossible. His acts might sometimes be beyond our grasp, but they are performed in perfect integrity, truth, and wisdom. Scripture says of God, "You have kept your promise because you are righteous" (Neh. 9:8 NIV).

> In His coming, He assured us of His unfailing goodness.

Love-Prompted

So there is a reason why God healed this man and others. It is so obvious that we miss it. God healed this man because He is like that. His reason is His nature. If we go to hear music, there's music in us. If we have to be dragged to a concert, there's no music in us. What we do spontaneously shows who we are. God never acts out of character. Healing this man shows His character.

Additionally, God is love and is love-prompted. A spontaneous outflow of free goodness is not to be traced to some eternal and mysterious sovereignty but is to be credited to Him. He came to bring light, to make the blind see and lead us. Giving eyes to this man tells us all we want to know. We understand Him.

I enjoy salvation, healing, the baptism in the Holy Spirit, and a thousand more realities. My religion must fit what I enjoy. I find it in the same Bible as did Jesus, Paul, Luther, Wesley, and company. Rationalists, liberal scholars, and their fellow nonbelievers offer me constantly shifting theological opinions. They can't accommodate and bear the weight of my experience.

They use the smear word *fundamentalist,* but what God has done can't be wiped off the record. They can't rewrite history. The "wise and prudent," as Jesus calls them, sit on the shore telling me it is worth nothing. Let them! I'm not the judge of that. I'm not going to jettison my faith, however plausible their advice.

John's great question remains, "To see or not to see?" Despite twenty million books in the British Museum Library, the mystery of life remains. For thousands of years, men's minds have tackled the great questions and are as far away from any answer as ever. God speaking through Isaiah complained of this, "Israel does not know, my people do not understand" (Isa. 1:3 NIV). God does not want us ignorant about the meanings of life. He Himself is the "why" of everything. The answers are a divine revelation, and they can never be received except by faith. Faith is the only possible way to "know." Faith is the infrared camera with a wide-angle lens. As finite humans, we walk in the darkness, but faith gives "night-sight" eyes.

The modern outlook has been influenced deeply by the Danish writer Søren Kierkegaard. Sadly, he describes faith as "a leap into the dark." Nonsense! It is a leap into the light. A greater writer, Paul the apostle, said, "He has delivered us from the power of darkness and conveyed us into the kingdom of the Son" (Col. 1:13).

John presented Jesus and everything related to Him as alive and active. Christian living is a daily, ongoing, believing experience. The true light now shines, but many pull down the blinds of unbelief and people grope around, always uncertain. Why squint in the gloom lit only by the flickering candles of human thought—brainpower before God's power?

Those who talk most of seeking the truth don't anticipate coming to any conclusion. They travel but don't expect to get anywhere. Jesus said, "He who seeks finds" (Luke 11:10), that is if they want to find. But some call themselves "agnostics" and on principle are people who deny they can know. I wonder how they *know* they can't know? The last thing they want is to find that the gospel is true. That is perhaps the most perverse of all attitudes.

Paul classified this as "always learning but never able to acknowledge the truth" (2 Tim. 3:7 NIV). John explained, "Men loved darkness rather than light, because their deeds were evil" (John 3:19). The blaze of glory and light that falls on those who believe may be too great to bear for the unclean. However, nobody ever came to Christ clean, but those who came all went on their way to paradise cleansed and forgiven.

chapter 11

Faith and My God

A woman was healed of an issue of blood (Luke 8:43–44) after secretly touching Christ and drawing on His healing virtue. He didn't know who had touched Him. When she came forward, He said to her, "Your faith has made you well" (Luke 8:48). His healing is simply available to any who make the faith contact.

Peter had to learn the same thing, even after being with Jesus for three years. **The contract of God with the human race contains a glorious nondiscrimination clause.** Peter met a Roman soldier and others with him, completely outside of Israel's territory, and found that God had answered his prayers. It astonished Peter, a strict Jew. He said, "I now realize how true it is that God does not show favoritism but accepts men from every nation who fear him and do what is right" (Acts 10:34–35 NIV).

> The contract of God with the human race contains a glorious nondiscrimination clause.

The Character of Christian Faith

That is the wonderful character of the Christian faith and of the Lord Himself. It is for the outsider. He met strangers and said, "Do not be afraid; only believe" (Mark 5:36). Otherwise, the price of admission into the kingdom and all its assets is nothing. The gospel gathers in and embraces everyone.

The Passport into the Kingdom

Faith is the passport, the visa, and the entry fee into the kingdom and all its resources. It is not by the rules of any organization. No one has a right to lord it over believers and bend them through some little door of their own into the blessings of God, dictating what their lives must be. There's no need. Faith alone is the opener, not a life conforming to someone's ideas of right and wrong. Some exercise this oppressive control and disguise it as care. We are each responsible for our own lives and cannot shuffle praise or blame onto someone else who told us what to do.

> Faith is the passport, the visa, and the entry fee into the kingdom.

The Cults

Religious groups that require personal submission to a leader are cults, not churches. A church contains all sorts of people at every degree of spiritual progress. The only pressure should be the exhortation to heed the Word of God. If church members begin to bow to a leader's personal orders, it is a creeping death. It is cultism. There is danger when any person is lifted up as having a higher than normal relationship with God. Jesus said that all are brothers.

A cult is a contradiction of the character of Christianity. Instead of faith, it substitutes obligations and obedience to the demands of the leaders. Liberty is the essence of Christ's gift to mankind. A cult is elitist, and Jesus and the gospel are all-embracing, all-inclusive, never exclusive.

Twice Jesus said, "One is your Master, even Christ" (Matt. 23:8, 10 KJV). Yet even He Himself, the true Master, never once interfered with the ordinary decisions of His followers. He left their own practical affairs to their own wisdom. Christ gave no orders, for He was not a dictator. He told no one where they should live or work, where they should go and when, what to do with their money or property, or whom they should marry. Disciples serve Christ with love. They would do anything for Him, but He never presumed or took advantage of it.

Disciples

We see an example of this in the book of Luke, chapter 12, when Jesus was speaking the parable of the rich fool: "Then one from the crowd said to Him, 'Teacher, tell my brother to divide the inheritance with me.' But He said to him, 'Man, who made Me a judge or an arbitrator over you?'" (vv. 13–14).

Look now at the original word *disciple* in Scripture. It means a "learner, or follower" and has nothing to do with discipline, regimentation, rules, or commands. Jesus only taught disciples and never "disciplined" anyone or imposed any penalty or pressure or threatened exclusion from the band of His followers. His comprehensive rule was simply, "He who is not with Me is against Me" (Luke 11:23). "Disciple" is not really an appropriate translation as it suggests "discipline," which is foreign to Christ's ideal. It is all of faith.

Christ can make us—we who otherwise would never make it. In the Gospels we see Him coming open-faced and open-armed. To Him, there were no nobodies, nor riffraff, no social rejects. He came for lost sheep. To women who were treated as subspecies in some Eastern countries, as they are even now, Christ gave ranking honor.

Jesus said, "I always do those things that please [the Father]" (John 8:29). What had He seen the Father do? He had seen Him stoop over the wretched tribes in Egypt, pick them up, and make them great.

Jesus did the same. He **chose fishermen, not princes, to be His ambassadors.** The Gospels show Him, again and again, meeting the unwanted and giving them a place. His outreach to the discarded is a moving part of the gospel story. Jesus is with the "lost" and the "last." The lost He finds, and to the last He says, "The last will be first" (Matt. 20:16). In Christ, everyone is someone, even the guilty thief on the cross. Christ never treated people as "the masses." To Him, we are all individuals, all special, and all loved.

> Jesus chose fishermen, not princes, to be His ambassadors.

Scripture aims at changing the nations of the whole world, but it mainly tells us of God's dealings with individuals such as Abraham, Jacob, Joseph, Moses, David, the kings, and the prophets. Jesus didn't preach sermons just hoping it would have a good, general effect. He chose people to get on with the task at hand. The Gospels spotlight many very ordinary individuals, even nameless folk, and they became keys to spiritual truth.

Everything of God Is Important

The point to note is this: God not only deals with us as individuals, He chooses us. He singles us out, just as He did Israel. All God does is important, never trivial or incidental. Everything in nature, down to the dancing particles of the atom, moves in accordance with an ultimate divine plan. The whole movement of creation works out the divine will. When we are chosen, it is the direct act of God intervening personally as part of His eternal process. It has that kind of significance. We have a vital place in the divine purpose. Faith puts us there.

Israel as a nation was chosen. Other nations were not, and they chose their god or gods, patronizing Baal, Ashteroth, Molech, or Ahmun. But Yahweh chose Israel, they did not choose Him. Israel was the people of God and belonged to Him. Other gods were the gods of nations and belonged to them, but they did not belong to their gods.

This is fact. It became living truth through Jesus Christ. Jesus said, "Ye have not chosen me, but I have chosen you" (John 15:16 KJV). He first loved us and set His love upon us. We belong to Him when He calls us and when we believe. Christ said, "My sheep hear My voice, and I know them. . . . They shall never perish; neither shall anyone snatch them out of My hand. My Father, who has given them to Me, is greater than all; and no one is able to snatch them out of My Father's hand" (John 10:27–29). The heathen keep their idols, but God keeps His people. Isaiah talks about the heathen carrying their idols, but quotes the Lord as saying, "Even to gray hairs I will carry you!" (46:4).

When we believe, we make living contact with a vital area of God. There are the common but wonderful areas in the heart of God—forgiveness, restoration, and salvation. But for each individual, there is also his or her own unique contact. **Each one who believes knows God in a way no one else does.** God is infinite. Aspects of His nature are endless. We can't know Him throughout His unfathomable depths. But every person is different, and we all came from God, shaped and molded, as He wants us, especially by the new birth, but "in His image." There is a bit of God just for us to know. We are connected with a little of His nature, which corresponds with our nature. In the ocean of God, there is a private mooring place for each of us alone and for no one else.

> Each one who believes knows God in a way no one else does.

The Personal God

It is hard for people to describe to others what God is like to them. God's greatness cannot be displayed through one life. It needs all our lives. We must all believe. Unless we all activate our faith, as we all can, then God's goodness is known in only limited fashion. It is through the church that the manifold riches of God are known to His praise and glory. God doesn't want one believer. He needs the millions so that His greatness can flow out. The goodness of God is a great jewel with a million facets, each flashing and burning. Every believer is equal, each touching some part of God's mind and heart for which God chose them, but all together we display the wonders of His grace.

By faith we discover our destiny in God. Not only does God express Himself by means of each of us, but also we ourselves only come fully alive as we touch Him by faith. There is something in God especially for me, when I believe. I was made by Him and for Him, not in some wide, general sense, but in an intimate, personal way.

God is *my* God. He was the God of Abraham who was close to Him in a different sense from Isaac, and Isaac was close to Him in a way Jacob was not. One can go through Scripture and see how people discovered God for themselves or, rather, how God revealed this or that side of His character to this one and that one. God was their God in a very personal sense.

There is a special part of each one of us that can only be satisfied when we come to God. The source of what we are made for is in Him. He reaches the depths and fundamentals of every heart. We shall never be contented by any other means. We can't substitute God. He designed us to respond to Him. He made us to be what we are, having a need, and that need was meant to be met only in God. He is, "*my* God," for each of us. Each man has a different nature with different thoughts, but Yahweh is Lord for each one's personality.

God is always what He is, but He is not a monolith. He is a living fountain of water. There is always freshness, a mystery for endless discovery and delight. There is no monotony in God. Whoever sees Him has a new view. Each of us discovers that what we are ourselves finds an echo in Him because we come from Him and we belong to Him as a child to its father. We see that in our new born-again nature, which is of God, not from earthly parentage. We find our home in Him. Our instinct responds to what He is. It is not a case of He loved *us,* but He loved *me* and gave Himself for *me.* I am that important "whosoever" of John 3:16. "I will give him a white stone, and on the stone a new name written which no one knows except him who receives it" (Rev. 2:17).

A whole area of the activity of God starts up when anyone begins to believe, because each one believes God in his own way. When we do not believe, there is a missing link in God's chain. We are not aliens, being given a visa to enter the kingdom. We are not gate-crashing. "The kingdom [was] prepared for you since the creation of the world," Jesus says in Matthew 25:34 (NIV). The Lord is not just a God, or the God, or even Abraham's God. He is *my* God. He presents Himself to each of us as individual personalities. When we come to God believing, it is like coming home.

> Each man and each woman has a special relationship with Christ that no one else can enter into.

We are not forcing our way into strange territory. Things have been waiting just for us, ready for when we begin to believe; everything has been set to go.

The Bible is not another history book of national events. It describes God's dealings with individuals like David, Daniel, Nathaniel, Lazarus, Nicodemus, and Simon Peter. There is no common relationship with Christ. **Each man and each woman has a special relationship with Christ that no one else can enter into.** It is a faith relationship. Each one believes God his way, according to God's plan. We see God our own way and believe in Him that way. We should not try to be a Paul, Wesley, or Wigglesworth. He asks us simply to believe, trust, and step out as He leads. The problems are all His. When we believe in His will, our faith is strengthened and shown.

His will is what Scripture teaches—that God isn't a weak force one day and a strong force another day. We need no barometer for God and no temperature gauge. He isn't around sometimes for revival or healing, but all the time—it is up to us, not God who never changes. He doesn't have moods.

The poet Matthew Arnold said, "The spirit bloweth and is still, / In mystery our soul abides." That is not true, but we temperamental people may experience it that way. The Pentecostal revival changed the old thinking of a God of revival spasms. He is the God of constant revival. He does not enter the field, because He never leaves it.

Changing the Church

This was the new Reformation, a doctrinal revelation changing the face of the church, like Martin Luther's justification by faith. This is the Holy Spirit by faith. The Spirit has come to abide and is not coming and going mysteriously. Jesus spoke of a constant wind, the Spirit "bloweth," not here today and gone tomorrow. God has no uncertainty factor, but our faith may be like that. The wind blew into the Upper Room on the Day of Pentecost and didn't stop. **All who set their sails of faith don't need to whistle for the wind, like men in the doldrums.** God has no doldrums.

Speaking of His "coming," both His constant coming and His second coming, here is something else that thrills me. His coming is given a special name in the New Testament—*Parousia*. It is called the "coming" of Jesus in our English Bibles in 1 Corinthians 15:23 and Matthew 24:3. But actually, *Parousia,* the biblical Greek word, means "presence." He will become *present*. The "presence of God" will fill the whole earth at His coming. That will be a notable thing—not a flash, being all over and done with, but the entire earth will become like the Upper Room on the Day of Pentecost. No one can escape or forget or ignore Him then.

> All who set their sails of faith don't need to whistle for the wind, like men in the doldrums.

Now, *presence* is a word not used in the Old Testament Hebrew. Instead, it has other words, like *face*. "LORD, lift up the light of Your countenance ["face" in Hebrew] upon us" (Ps. 4:6). He shone upon them from heaven. They did not seem to think of His presence as Christians do today, though they believed He could be on their side, perhaps by sending an angel to help.

But today we have only a misty idea of *Parousia*. God's presence is with us when He fulfills the promise of being where two or three are gathered together (Matt. 18:20). Then He is truly in our midst. The blessing and joy of such occasions, which to us seem more powerful sometimes than others, help us to prepare for that great consummation of faith when His presence fills earth and sky.

The Great Hope

God told Moses he could not see His face, that is, the glory of His presence. Yet Moses spoke to God, the Bible says, "face to face, as a man speaks to his friend" (Ex. 33:11). Whatever that was like, it was not the fullness of God's glory. In fact, when Moses said to God, "Show me Your glory" (Ex. 33:18), the Lord told him it was impossible for a person to live in that presence. However, we have seen "the glory of God in the face of Jesus Christ" (2 Cor. 4:6), though "through a glass, darkly; but then face to face" (1 Cor. 13:12 KJV). One of the last great promises of God in the Bible is in Revelation 22:4, "They shall see His face." That is the fulfillment of the promise of Christ, "Blessed are the pure in heart, / For they shall see God" (Matt. 5:8).

We shall see Him in His glory.

This is the great hope. It is not merely that we shall live forever or that the earth will be our paradise. Our expectation is to see the glorious, radiant face of our Lord Jesus Christ, which Moses could not see. **We shall see Him in His glory.**

Today, His presence is resurrection-active, a life-building energy passing into us. We are constantly in His presence, not just when we pray. He made that clear when He promised that He would never leave us nor forsake us. It is not the full glory to come, but it is no ordinary presence even now.

Many a time, I am conscious of Jesus Christ close to me as I speak for Him in our Gospel Crusades. It has been as if I saw Him walk from the platform among the crowd wherever people were reaching out for Him. He did and does wonders of salvation, restoration, and healing.

When our faith rises, we have a sense of His presence no human contact can ever surpass. A friend may be with us and even embrace us. But the presence of Christ means He pours Himself toward us, upon us, pervading our whole being with an active, dynamic effect.

A Visitation from God

Jesus never uses the language of visitation. He said, "Where two or three are gathered together in My name, I am there in the midst of them" (Matt. 18:20). He did not say, "there I will be," but, "there I am," using the great "I AM" name of God, indicating changeless permanence. We need not wait for Him. He is actively here, waiting for us. God never comes as a visitor. God never says, "Oh, I see a few believers; they're praying. I'll go and be with them." He doesn't come to us; we come to Him.

We use the phrase "a visitation of God" as if He came as a hurricane or as if He had just been passing by and dropped in on us like a whirlwind for a day or so. I can't find any Scripture indicating that God works that way. God never talks like that, and He doesn't promise it. **Jesus said that when the Spirit comes, He will "abide" with us,** like the sun always shining, always at zenith. "THE LORD IS THERE"— Yahweh Shammah (Ezek. 48:35).

> Jesus said that when the Spirit comes, He will "abide" with us.

So then, what are these experiences we have when He seems to come to us?

Perhaps it is not "seems" at all. The truth is, we isolate ourselves and protect ourselves from His coming. We put up a windshield, quench the Spirit, and block His access. We have desires that clash with His will, mainly because our desires may not always be in line with His will—His very best for us.

The Word

Look again at this well-known verse in Revelation 3:20: "Behold, I stand at the door and knock. If anyone hears My voice and opens the door, I will come in to him and dine with him." The biblical Greek words are, "I will enter to him." Now, let me explain that the word *to* is special (Greek, *pros*). It has the suggestion of "movement toward." It can be translated "with." When we hear Christ at the door and we open our lives to Him, He comes *with* us.

The famous first verse of John's Gospel says, "The Word was with God." This uses the same special preposition *(pros)*. The Word was "with" God. That is, **there is always a constant movement in God of active fellowship,** directed toward Him and moving into Him infinitely.

This is a picture of God as a glorious living Being, Father, Son, and Spirit. We name it but never understand and shall not until we see Him. We can think of two glorious fountains of light forever cascading toward one another, each one lost in the other. We should say *three* cascades, for the Holy Spirit is also in that glorious, everlasting triple fountain of life. To dwell in this presence is

> There is always a constant movement in God of active fellowship.

the final reward of faith. We believe for it and shall at last have it.

That is what we are talking about when we say God is "with us." Jesus prayed, "That they may be one as we are one" (John 17:22 NIV). The Bible word is *fellowship,* one with Him. It is a mutual reaction, a loving oneness, like that of the Father and the Son through the Holy Spirit. The same Spirit who is the bond in the Godhead comes to bond us to the Father and the Son.

In John 14:18 Jesus says, "I will come to you." It is the present tense, "I am coming to you"—that is what is happening all the time. Jesus said more than that, for He included the Father and Holy Spirit. John 14:23 says, "If anyone loves Me . . . We will come to him and make Our home with him." That present coming is happening all over the world— the Holy Spirit is falling in the former and latter rain together ceaselessly. The true reward of faith is not to get some money or material benefit from God, but to be One with Him and see His glory.

What God tells us about Himself is a prophecy of what He will do. All God's acts are precedents or rehearsals for regular performances. What He has shown us, by His own spontaneous initiative, is to encourage our faith to ask and believe.

For instance, the two miracle prophets, Elijah and Elisha, both raised mothers' sons from the dead (1 Kings 17 and 2 Kings 4). These are the two outstanding healing miracles of the Old Testament. About seven hundred years later, Jesus went into the same area and did the same thing, raising a mother's son in the entrance to Nain (Luke 7).

> What God tells us about Himself is a prophecy of what He will do.

Now, notice something very striking that happened with those miracles. Elijah and Elisha and Jesus not only all raised sons from the dead, but they all gave the sons back to their mothers. It was a kind of hallmark or fingerprint. To raise a son and give him back to his mother, rather than the father, showed the same Lord was at work in the same way. Seven centuries made no difference, and twenty centuries make no difference, either. He works wonders on earth because He is on familiar territory, doing what He did before.

Faith doesn't stand alone. It **gets things going,** begins with things happening. It opens the door, sets the sails, clears the decks, and makes the way for God. It is not a case of God one day waking up and starting to do things. He waits only for us to dare to do in His name by faith what He revealed of His goodness and promise in the past. John 5:17 states it perfectly: "My Father," Christ said, "is always at his work to this very day, and I, too, am working" (NIV).

What God was and did spells out His will for the present and future. It is for our faith to grasp it, act upon it, and bring to bear God's wonder-working power again upon the world. His past predicts the present—if we believe.

> **Faith gets things going.**

There is perfect harmony and consistency in God from eternity to eternity. And it is that eternity that has swept down upon us earthlings and will carry us along in His everlasting joy.

chapter 12

Faith and Prayer

Prayer is not an interview with God that terminates when you say, "Amen." It doesn't mean, "So long, Lord!" As the Bible stresses, He is as much with you when you are not praying as when you are. The book of Joshua, chapter 1, is a prime example. In it, God says, "No man shall be able to stand before you all the days of your life; as I was with Moses, so I will be with you. I will not leave you nor forsake you" (v. 5). His presence is with those who love Him and is unconditional.

In the Midst of Us

When we gather together, someone probably prays, "Lord, be present here today! Be among us!" Is this necessary? He said, "Where two or three are gathered together in My name, I am there in the midst of them" (Matt. 18:20). "Be with us, Lord!" almost suggests He will not be with us unless He is pressured to take notice, as some of Baal's followers tried with Baal on Mount Carmel. Is this faith? Faith believes the Word of Christ. **Faith does not ask Christ to fulfill promises** that are unconditional. Faith takes it as done, as actualized.

He does not say, "I will come in their midst," but "I am in their midst." He does not come into a gathering of worshipers so we can say at a certain point, "God has come among us!" He is not drawn there by our fervency or when we work up the "right atmosphere." In fact, He does not come into our presence. We must come into His presence, "Unto him shall the gathering of the people be" (Gen. 49:10 KJV). That is His name—Yahweh Shammah, "the Lord is there." He is the "Alpha," always the beginning. He is not a will-o'-the-wisp, an elusive spirit, hard to catch, here today and gone tomorrow. No techniques are needed, no formula to generate His presence. We can obliterate the fact of His presence from our view by our fog of doubt, just as the vast, rocky mass of Mount Everest can disappear behind a cloud bank.

> Faith does not ask Christ to fulfill promises.

His Promises

At times, though, His promise is misunderstood. It does not mean two or three are needed for His presence, but that His presence is the important factor when we do meet. He is there then, not just when we have achieved perfect harmony. It is Christ that takes priority. He is the head of the church, the pastor is not. He is the chief of the church board, the chairman is not. Christ is the head of the home.

This promise of Christ to be among us can also be taken as a warning. He is Lord of the church. When there is bickering, politics, intrigue, envy, place and position seeking, animosity, or outright quarreling, He is still there. If Christians gather as Christians, He is with them whether it is convenient or not. There's no getting rid of Him! There is simply nothing we can do about it. **We didn't ask Him to come, and we can't ask Him to leave.** We can only reckon on it, take advantage, or take warning of it as Scripture says: "They that feared the LORD spake often one to another: and the LORD hearkened, and heard it, and a book of remembrance was written before him" (Mal. 3:16 KJV).

> He does not say, "I will come in their midst," but "I am in their midst."

That passage of Scripture concerns our relationships with one another, as when one offends another and forgiveness is needed. What happens then happens in the sight of Christ Himself. It concerns two who come together to sort out their differences, with perhaps a third party as arbitrator. Christ is still to be recognized as the chief One present. Then, "whatever you bind on earth will be bound in heaven" (Matt. 18:18). That verse has nothing whatsoever to do with the casting out of demons, for demons are not in mind in the entire chapter. Rather, it has everything to do with a forgiving attitude.

> We didn't ask Him to come, and we can't ask Him to leave.

It follows that where faith grasps the promise of Christ and knows He is present, then all false attitudes and animosity wither away. **Faith is the key to peace and harmony.** And faith in God means faith in a present God, not a remote God who must be called back from some distant heaven. We worship a Lord who is always with us. We speak of "going to meet God in worship," in church, at a given time. If we only worship Him, then it doesn't reach Old Testament levels, never mind New Testament revelations. Jesus said we would neither in this place nor that place worship the Father (John 4:21). We don't

> Faith is the key to peace and harmony.

"meet with God" as if keeping an appointment, trusting He will turn up. He has not been in the next street all day. Paul said, "I bow my knees to the Father of our Lord Jesus Christ" (Eph. 3:14). Paul did not mean that was the way he usually worshiped, but that was the way he lived. He lived worshiping Christ. Worship in Bible terms never was an occasional event but a permanent attitude.

The Attitude of Prayer

Praying doesn't create God's presence. We pray because God *is* present. If He were not present, our prayer would only reach the ceiling, not the throne. And He is fully there, not just the finger of God or the face of God or a dim light shining. The idea has been suggested that the more we pray, the greater the intensity of God's power and presence. Someone once wrote that the power of God is in exact proportion to the time spent praying for it. No such suggestion is found anywhere in Scripture. Indeed, after the baptism in the Spirit, there is never any suggestion that we pray for power. Charles Spurgeon called the presence of Christ "the Christian's only Certainty."

In the book of Acts, Peter and John were going to pray, and healed a cripple on the way without first praying for him:

> A certain man lame from his mother's womb was carried, whom they laid daily at the gate of the temple which is called Beautiful, to ask alms from those who entered the temple; who, seeing Peter and John about to go into the temple, asked for alms. And fixing his eyes on him, with John, Peter said, "Look at us." So he gave them his attention, expecting to receive something from them. Then Peter said, "Silver and gold I do not have, but what I do have I give you: In the name of Jesus Christ of Nazareth, rise up and walk." And he took him by the right hand and lifted him up, and immediately his feet and ankle bones received strength. So he, leaping up, stood and walked and entered the temple with them—walking, leaping, and praising God. (Acts 3:2–8)

They were able to heal the man before praying because Christ was with them, and they acted in faith (Acts 3:6, 16).

Faith that God is with us inspires us to pray. It is natural to want to speak to Him when we know He is listening. When people do not pray, it is because they don't believe He is listening. Jesus prayed *because* He had such a perfect and immediate awareness of His Father. He said, "Father, I thank You that

> **Faith that God is with us inspires us to pray.**

You have heard me. And I know that You always hear Me" (John 11:41–42). Sometimes the Scripture doesn't even say Jesus prayed but that He just lifted His head and "said."

Faith without prayer is possible, but prayer without faith is useless. Jesus said, "When ye pray, believe" (Mark 11:24 KJV). It is the prayer of faith that is effective. Prayer is not a sigh of desperation but an act of victorious faith. To turn toward God and speak to Him is a victory in itself. On that victory other victories are built.

Faith, as is noted, is the vital principle of prayer. So, once we have believed, can we stop praying and just leave it at that? Does praying the prayer of faith mean we move on and don't bother anymore? Isn't it a sign of unbelief to pray again? The answer is that faith is not something you switch on for five minutes when you make a request to God. **The prayer of faith sets up a faith situation.** You are standing before God. You stay in that situation or relationship until the prayer is finally answered.

The instruction is, "Pray without ceasing" (1 Thess. 5:17). That does not mean 24 hours a day and 365 days a year and everlastingly trying to think of something to pray about. It means don't quit, never let up in your appeal to God once you begin.

> The prayer of faith sets up a faith situation.

Continuing to pray is not a sign of unbelief, but of faith. In fact, you prove you believe by keeping on praying. The Gospel of Luke records that "men always ought to pray and not lose heart" (18:1).

James 5:7–8 speaks of the need for patient faith. "Therefore be patient, brethren, until the coming of the Lord. See how the farmer waits for the precious fruit of the earth, waiting patiently for it until it receives the early and latter rain. You also be patient. Establish your hearts, for the coming of the Lord is at hand."

And when we turn to the record of Elijah's prayer for rain (1 Kings 18), he did not ask, believe, and let it go at that. To begin with, he acted in faith by telling the king there would be rain. He said to go have a meal and be ready because there was going to be storm (18:41). Then he went up to the top of Carmel, cast himself down on the ground, crouching with his head between his knees in an attitude of waiting. It doesn't actually say he prayed. Maybe he said no words. Prayer can be wordless because "the Spirit Himself makes intercession for us with groanings which cannot be uttered" (Rom. 8:26).

Elijah simply waited in a childlike attitude of trust. He told a servant to let him know when the clouds appeared. The servant climbed to a high ridge seven times, each time seeing nothing until the last time, and then a small cloud appeared that indicated a storm. So far as Elijah was concerned he was simply waiting. He had his foot in the door of heaven so it wouldn't shut. If the servant had needed to go up fifty times, he would still have waited. That is the patience and persistence of faith.

Tremendous Patience

James gives us another illustration—the patience of Job. In what way was Job patient? Many have said that he was patient with his sufferings. The third chapter of Job in no way sounds like that. It begins, "After this Job opened his mouth and cursed the day of his birth. And Job spoke, and said, 'May the day perish on which I was born, / And the night in which it was said, / "A male child is conceived."'" He continues in this strain for twenty-six verses in which one thing is very prominently missing—any sign of patience with suffering.

In fact, the Bible as a whole does not display marked toleration of suffering. Unlike all other religions, which demand resignation, Bible faith protests against illnesses and pains. In the first five books of the New Testament—more than half of it—**Jesus led an attack upon physical suffering as the work of the devil.** Christ displayed no patience with the world's misery.

Job's patience was not with his afflictions but with God. This great man showed not a flicker of mistrust in that direction. Puzzlement, yes; questions, yes; frustration, yes; but not agitated criticism of God. He used some of the greatest phrases

> Jesus led an attack upon physical suffering as the work of the devil.

we know: "When He has tested me, I shall come forth as gold"; "Let come on me what may! . . . Though He slay me, yet will I trust Him"; "I know that my redeemer liveth . . . and though . . . worms destroy this body, yet in my flesh shall I see God" (23:10; 13:13, 15; 19:25–26 KJV). The Lord later spoke saying that Job had spoken the thing that is right of Him (42:7).

Many ask about sickness and suffering. Why does God permit it? Why hasn't God healed this one yet? What is wanted is a healing, not an explanation. Explanations don't help very much if we have a toothache! Job gives us the true answer to suffering—faith—keep believing God. But we need patience, which is the quality of faith.

Not only James, but Jesus also spoke of the patience of faith. In Luke 18, a judge who neither bothered about God nor man brushed aside a widow who needed justice. But she kept coming back until he decided he had better deal with her or she would never stop pestering him.

Jesus said that if an unjust judge would act like that, how much more would God "avenge His own elect, who cry out day and night to Him, though He bears long with them?" (Luke 18:7). This does not compare God with an unjust judge who can be persuaded by sheer importunity. It simply means that after we have prayed we need patience, patient continuance in well-doing.

God Always Hears

"Patience" is used 32 times in the New Testament, as just one of many expressions encouraging our perseverance in faith and prayer. Romans 12:12 says we should be "rejoicing in hope, patient in tribulation, continuing steadfastly in prayer." God is patient with us. The Lord is "the God of patience" (Rom. 15:5), and 2 Thessalonians 3:5 speaks of "the patience of Christ."

God always hears prayer. He **hears every time we move our lips.** He doesn't send us an acknowledgment, such as, "Your prayer is heard and is receiving attention." It may seem He isn't listening or doing anything. We should "cry day and night to Him," as Jesus said, but we should display ordinary confidence in Him not to let us down. Healings don't take place

> God hears every time we move our lips.

when people have to crank up their faith to spark off a brief flash or when faith flops into a healing service half dead.

People come who are sick and have prayed but have not been healed. God has heard their prayers, but is waiting for a real live link of faith to connect to His power. The Lord chooses whom He wills to provide that link. Healing follows, not always through the evangelist's prayer, but though the prayers that God has already heard.

Faith is given to us because we live in the dimension of time, not in eternity, and because God has to take the time factor into account when performing His wonders. They may not always be instant. But a persistent living faith, pressing through in prayer is, of course, waiting to be drawn from.

Is it possible, however, to pray ourselves out of faith? Yes, if our prayers are more expressions of worry than acts of "faith triumphant." We can pray ourselves out of faith if we didn't really believe in the first place. Prayer does not generate faith. The increase of faith comes from the Word of God as the Spirit opens

> Faith is given to us because we live in the dimension of time, not in eternity.

it to our hearts, not as we learn it from books. Faith is not a surgical implant from the celestial world. If we have real faith at the start, it does not need to get better. It will not get worse by praying if we began without any!

The one thing Scripture is most positive about is that God always hears prayer. However, that does not mean He must always acquiesce as if He were afraid of offending us. He is not there to do our will. **We are here only so that His will may be done.** He is the Lord God, maker of heaven and earth, not the genie of the lamp to say the right words and have Him bound to dance and attend on us. There's no miracle in words, in mouthing a certain formula, as do the heathen, or in using the name of Jesus like a mantra. They that fear Him will be heard.

An Act of Faith

Can prayer, in certain instances, run up against a shut door? A prime instance is in 2 Kings 4, the story of the "great woman of Shunem."

She was great for only one reason—her faith. Her husband was not wealthy—he worked in the fields. The king or the head of the Israelite army did not know her (v. 13). Her vision was far greater. She was far happier to be known by Elisha the man of God. He was her kind. She "belonged to that lot" as the world often calls believers. The alternative "lot" will pay $100,000 to sit at the same table as royalty. The great woman didn't even want the king's notice, nor that of the top army brass.

> We are here only so that His will may be done.

She was like many today, who travel hundreds of miles to meet a real man of God but wouldn't bother to look out the window to see a much-married Hollywood film star across the street. Faith totally elevated this great woman's scale of values and interests. She sought out and had eyes only for true greatness, which is always of God, and she was rewarded.

In answer to faith, God gave her one son (v. 17). When he was still a boy he went with his father to the field at harvesttime and possibly had a sunstroke. A man brought him back to his mother, but at noon he died in her arms.

Now began the patience and process of faith by two people, the woman and the prophet. First, she put him on the prophet's bed, "shut the door upon him, and went out" (v. 21). We are told in 2 Kings 13:21 that a dead man rose to life when the corpse was put in the tomb of Elijah, but nothing happened for the woman's little boy when he was put on the living prophet's bed. But she put the dead child there with living faith. The Bible emphasizes the fact that she shut the door. She shut it on the fact of death and opened her heart to the fact of Almighty God.

The Great Door of Faith

It is the "door of faith," as Acts 14:27 calls it. Christ gave us a hint of something special in mentioning a door (Matt. 6:6): "But you, when you pray, go into your room, and when you have shut your door, pray to your Father who is in the secret place; and your Father who sees in secret will reward you openly." That is a revelation about God—He is "in the secret place." That is where God is. **The door of faith is the only way to access Him.** In John 14:19, Jesus said, "The world will see Me no more, but you will see Me." Earlier He said, "I am with you for only a short time, and then I go to the one who sent me. You will look for me, but you will not find me; and where I am, you cannot come" (John 7:33–34 NIV). God is found in the secret place, not sitting around wherever, accessible to any casual passerby.

> The door of faith is the only way to access Him.

When the Shunammite woman shut the door, it was a recognition that there was a way to reach out to God. That room represented Elisha, and Elisha represented the Lord. The shut door for all believers carries the same significance— it is a symbol of a "secret" world, unknown to the unbelieving world. God has not disappeared. He waits behind the closed door, and in our hand is the key to open it—faith.

She asked her husband to saddle the donkey so she could go to the man of God quickly. He asked why, but she said, "It's all right" (2 Kings 4:23 NIV). All right? But her son was dead! How could she say that and not even tell her husband! She believed, but he wouldn't and might have interfered with the faith process.

Elisha recognized her coming and sent Gehazi to ask her, "Is your child all right?" Elisha knew how precious the boy was to his mother. To Gehazi, she would say nothing. She had infinitely more trust in God, whom she could not see, than in this man

> The devil will always try to push you away from where your hope is.

whom she could see. She did not commit herself to him and remarked, "Everything is all right!" (v. 26 NIV). Her simple conviction was that because of God it was all right. She came to Elisha, but Gehazi tried to push her away—**the devil will always try to push you away from where your hope is.** Then the prophet admitted the Lord had revealed nothing to him as to her trouble. There was no previous supernatural link to build up any expectations.

When Elisha knew the boy was dead he sent his own staff with Gehazi to lay upon the child's face. This was similar to sending a handkerchief to a sick person whom we can't reach. The woman had no faith in that, even if Elisha did, but only because she didn't trust Gehazi. She refused to leave Elisha. The prophet at that point got up and followed her, and they met Gehazi returning, saying there was no sound or response when he placed the staff on the boy's face. He was not awakened. Time had obviously passed.

Elisha eventually reached the house, and we are told that he saw the child "lying dead on his couch." He went in and he also "shut the door on the two of them and prayed" (vv. 32–33 NIV). The bed and the staff had worked no wonder. Now what? He tried again, getting on top of the boy till the child's cold flesh became warm; but natural warmth brought no life. Only God, not Elisha, could transfer His life to the boy. Elisha next got up and walked up and down—more praying, and still nothing.

He had done everything possible. So, what should he do? Open that closed door and say, "I'm sorry, madam, but it looks useless, I've done everything I know that usually works, but the Lord has taken your boy." Yes? In fact, no! He simply did what he did before, stretching himself on the boy—and "the child sneezed seven times, and . . . opened his eyes" (v. 35).

Until then, Elisha had allowed no one behind that shut door. Now, he called Gehazi, and Gehazi called the mother. "She went in, fell at his feet, and bowed to the ground; then she picked up her son and went out" (v. 37)—that is, out of the death chamber and out of the prophet's own room.

Believing God, the woman refused to accept the death of her son. He had been born to her by Elisha's word of knowledge (vv. 15–16). He could not be taken from her. She had grounds for her faith when she saw him dead. But she would not look on the boy dead anymore—she "shut the door," until he was in her arms, alive, as she believed to see.

That woman had incredible faith even when the child died on her lap. Elisha expected a swift response—faith was positive all the way through. For neither Elisha nor the Shunammite was it a matter of a routine act of faith. They carried on doing what they should behind that closed door until God answered.

How many prayers are not answered because people stop praying too soon? They make an experimental gesture or two with no great expectations of suc-cess. If things don't come crackling into life, they want no fur-

> The Door opens at even a child's touch of faith.

ther bother; they will find somebody else to help instead of God. The reason why so many older folks are found in church is that they have had time to search and discover that there is nobody else to help, and there is but one door and only one.

There is a way to God and that is through Christ **the Door,** and that Door **opens at even a child's touch of faith.** It is as we read in Revelation 3:7–8: "What he opens no one can shut, and what he shuts no one can open. . . . See, I have placed before you an open door that no one can shut" (NIV)—that is, no one unless he possesses that key called faith.

chapter 13

Faith in the Name of Jesus

The gods were always disassociated from the lives of the pagans. The gods were always parasites, demanding much but giving nothing. The pagans feared their gods and didn't trust them. For Israel, trust in the Lord was their life stance. Jesus Christ, to Christians, means even more—**faith in Him is their soul's spiritual lifeblood;** it is in constant circulation.

When we begin believing in the name of Jesus, we are not just "believers." We are repositioned; it is a personality shift or transfer. We are not just club members, standing up to be counted for Jesus. We are placed *inside* of what His name represents. We live in Him, inside of all He did. Believers become something very special, and it comes from what Christ is. We don't know what all that is at present, but as the book of 1 John reveals, we will:

> Faith in Him is their soul's spiritual lifeblood.

Behold what manner of love the Father has bestowed on us, that we should be called children of God! Therefore the world does not know us, because it did not know Him. Beloved, now we are children of God; and it has not yet been revealed what we shall be, but we know that when He is revealed, we shall be like Him, for we shall see Him as He is. And everyone who has this hope in Him purifies himself, just as He is pure. (3:1–3)

This is most impacting, for the Bible says we have been placed into God's family. **For a sinful person to become a child of God, a miraculous transformation must take place.** This is accomplished when we give our lives to Christ.

Effects of Faith

Some effects of faith are already evident. Faith makes life rational—it adds up. The experience is liberating, like orphans finding their father, or the condemned being reprieved, like light scattering darkness. The endless, empty darkness of eternity is filled with warm sunshine.

The world may say, "What's in a name?" In several instances that has been discussed, but now comes the highest name of all. What's in Jesus' name? We begin to find out by looking again at the great name of God, the Lord

> For a sinful person to become a child of God, a miraculous transformation must take place.

(Yahweh). Israel held that name as sacred and awesome. At the beginning, it was only a title, like a sealed book. They didn't know what was in it. It held the mystery of God's very being, a holy secret. Even Moses had to ask what it was. God's answer was, "I am who I am."

But God made known His ways unto Moses, and His acts unto the children of Israel. The Psalms clarify this further. For example, in David's Psalm 103, he blessed the Lord and realized much.

> Bless the LORD, O my soul;
> And all that is within me, bless His holy name!
> Bless the LORD, O my soul,
> And forget not all His benefits:
> Who forgives all your iniquities,
> Who heals all your diseases,
> Who redeems your life from destruction,
> Who crowns you with lovingkindness and tender
>   mercies,
> Who satisfies your mouth with good things,
> So that your youth is renewed like the eagle's. (vv. 1–5)

Line upon line, fold by fold, the Lord opened His glory to Israel. Name was added to name, but His greatest name had yet to be known. It would not be a mere title or a mystery, but a great explanation. It would not be known until it was understood in all its wonder, height, and depth. It was the name of Jesus that David was describing.

Philippians 2:9–11 states, "God also has . . . given Him the name which is above every name; that at the name of Jesus every knee should bow, of those in heaven, and of those on earth, and of those under the earth; and that **every** tongue should confess that Jesus Christ is Lord, to the glory of God the Father."

The gospel is not a theological doctrine. Mark 1:1 calls it "the gospel [good news] of Jesus Christ." It is not some good news about Him. One can have good news about people, about their successes or good fortune. But they themselves are not news. In contrast, Jesus *is* news—not history. He is the world's most alive news. He makes news every hour. Jesus is not only a historical figure but the greatest Person alive today.

> "Every tongue should confess that Jesus Christ is Lord."

The gospel, the good news, is the good news *of* Jesus. He is the good news. We have faith in Him, not only in what He said or doctrines about Him. He is not a proposition, but our great Friend. Books have been written about God as "the ground of our being." That is not Jesus. The Jesus millions know is a warm presence, with a living hand stretched out to save, comfort, and encourage.

The book of Hebrews begins, "[God] has spoken to us by his Son" (1:2 NIV). It means God has spoken to us about Himself and immediately goes on talking about who He is. God's message to us is about Himself, not just about morals or ultimate purposes. The Bible is not for philosophic and intellectual interest but is a book aimed at creating a love situation between God and His chosen people. Everything is in Him. He is the Beginning and Ending, the fountain of reality. His name, Jesus, crystallizes a million blessings.

Jesus was "a teacher . . . come from God" (John 3:2), as Nicodemus saw, but His teaching always centered on Himself and went back to Himself. He said, "The Scriptures . . .

testify of Me" (John 5:39). His message was, "Come unto Me
. . . learn of Me"—that is, "get to know Me."

Jesus said, "He who has seen Me has seen the Father"
(John 14:9). If the Father is like Jesus, then God is more wonderful than anyone has ever thought or read. Israel had their
wonderful knowledge of God, but Jesus lifted it to the sev-
enth heaven. We spoke of the names of the Lord, such as
Yahweh Jirah, but the name of Jesus is higher than every
other name, because it includes them all. Even the apostles
knew this, as evidenced by Scripture.

> Let it be known to you all. And to all the people of
> Israel, that by the name of Jesus Christ of Nazareth,
> whom you crucified, whom God raised from the
> dead, by Him this man stands here before you whole.
> This is the "stone which was rejected by you
> builders, which has become the chief cornerstone."
> Nor is there salvation in any other, for there is no
> other name under heaven given among men by which
> we must be saved. (Acts 4:10–12)

Whatever the Yahweh names declared about God, Jesus
is. Hebrews 1:3 states He was the "express image" of God's
Being. One translation says, "the representation of the reality" of God and another says,
"the radiance of God's glory."
If God is like Jesus, the
Almighty is not an unfeeling

Jesus is God in action.

obelisk in a faraway heaven. He could not rest on the throne
when things were wrong down here. He had to come and do
something about it. **Jesus is God in action;** so is the Holy
Spirit.

The first Christian martyr, Stephen, is a prime example of God in action. When he preached to the council about Jesus, he enraged the officials, and they took him out and stoned him to death. But before he died, he had much to say:

"You stiff-necked and uncircumcised in heart and ears! You always resist the Holy Spirit; as your fathers did, so do you. Which of the prophets did your fathers not persecute? And they killed those who foretold the coming of the Just One, of whom you now have become the betrayers and murderers, who have received the law by the direction of angels and have not kept it." When they heard these things they were cut to the heart, and they gnashed at him with their teeth. But he, being full of the Holy Spirit, gazed into heaven and saw the glory of God, and Jesus standing at the right hand of God, and said, "Look! I see the heavens opened and the Son of Man standing at the right hand of God!" Then they cried out with a loud voice, stopped their ears, and ran at him with one accord; and they cast him out of the city and stoned him. And the witnesses laid down their clothes at the feet of a young man named Saul. And they stoned Stephen as he was calling on God and saying, "Lord Jesus, receive my spirit." Then he knelt down and cried out with a loud voice, "Lord, do not charge them with this sin." And when he had said this, he fell asleep. (Acts 7:51–60)

When this first Christian martyr lifted up his eyes, he saw Jesus standing, not sitting, by the right hand of God. The Lord had risen to receive him.

The Son Is the Father

When Jesus came, we saw what God's glory was. On this earth a man's glory is what he does or makes. An artist's glory is a great painting. An engineer's glory is a great bridge. God's glory is His works, not just the Shekinah, the divine flame illuminating the Holy of Holies or the shattering spectacle of a trembling Mount Sinai. His glory was His labor and love, selflessness and sacrifice, humility and obedience. Most of all, to Him the Cross was His glory, as He tells us throughout the last chapters of John's Gospel.

"God the Son" means "God the Father"; He is not an inscrutable Being wrapped up in Himself—a solo God—but a wonderful Godhead, the thrice holy Tri-unity, in everlasting interaction, eternal communion, ceaseless love, and fellowship radiating love throughout all creation.

When we believe in the name of Jesus, we believe all that is in it. A child can name His name to begin mighty events. One fact is too wonderful not to be true: that the Son of God became the Son of Man. It is impossible in human thought. If people can't believe it, they certainly

> When we believe in the name of Jesus, we believe all that is in it.

could not invent it. Unless it happened, it would never have crossed anyone's mind. No one who has not heard of it ever thought or dreamed of it. To be spoken of, it had to happen. The truth is beyond us. We can only stand back in wonder and worship.

It was God's experience only. We cannot enter into it. More than His becoming man is the overwhelming fact that

He died as man. God experienced death. The "Prince of life" tasted death for all men. What that was like, mortals could never know.

In the Name of Jesus

People cannot possibly appreciate the amazing privilege of believing and praying in the name of Jesus unless they meditate on that background.

The Old and New Testaments explain each other, and like two witnesses, declare what His name is. The importance is not the mere word itself, but it is the code word for the activity of God on earth and more yet to be done and known.

His name—Jesus—was decided before He came to earth (Matt. 1:21). It was a common human name—others were called Jesus (Acts 13:6) or Joshua. To be one of us and one with us (Immanuel), Jesus took human nature and a human name. It shows Him to be a member of our race. He belongs to us here, and He will come back here where He was born. He is "the Man Christ Jesus" forever (1 Tim. 2:5; Heb. 13:8).

Name as a word is written more than one thousand times in Scripture. It shows names were spiritually important. Seven reasons why people received their names have been listed in Scripture. Several of them are behind the naming of Jesus. His name was given, according to Matthew 1:21,

- to fulfill prophecy;
- to give Him human identity;
- to link man with God;

- to represent the salvation as the work of God;

- to signify new spiritual understanding;

- and because "He shall save His people from their sins."

Some names were prophecies. For example Isaiah used whole sentences for his children. One was named, "Maher-Shalal-Hash-Baz" (Isa. 8:1), meaning, "Speed the spoil. Hasten the prey." But the name of Jesus was not a prophecy. It was a fulfillment of prophecy. In Him, all prophecy came to a head and was consummated. He was the One who should come (Luke 24:25–27). The first name in the New Testament is "Jesus," because **the New Testament is prophecy being fulfilled.**

Names were sometimes changed when a person changed. Abram became Abraham, Jacob became Israel, and Naomi said, "Call me Mara." It commemorated their new experience. Saul of Tarsus, the man whose hero was the proud King Saul, became the humble "Paul" when he met Jesus.

However, the name of Jesus never changed. No experience changed Him. He came to save His people from their sins, and He did. Though the name of Jesus was never altered, two titles were added. After His triumph on the cross, Peter announced in Jerusalem, "God has made this Jesus . . . both Lord and Christ" (Acts 2:36). Jesus is His personal name. Lord is His rank and office. Christ is His work as the One anointed to set the captives free (Isa. 61:1).

> The New Testament is prophecy being fulfilled.

Jesus is the Hebrew name, Joshua (Yehosua shortened to Yeshua). It means "the Lord (is) salvation." It is hidden in

Isaiah 62:11, "Say to the daughter of Zion, / 'See, your Savior comes!'"(NIV) or "your Yeshua comes." Jesus means Savior.

Anyone who talks about Jesus or Christianity without salvation talks nonsense. Salvation is what Jesus means. The living heart of the Christian faith is that through this Man is preached the forgiveness of sin.

> "By Him everyone who believes is justified from all things."

The thirteenth chapter of the book of Acts explains it further: "He whom God raised up saw no corruption. Therefore let it be known to you, brethren, that through this Man is preached to you the forgiveness of sins; and **by Him everyone who believes is justified from all things** from which you could not be justified by the law of Moses" (vv. 37–39).

Making It Crystal Clear

Believing in Jesus' name is the same as believing in Him because His name crystallizes what He is. In the Psalms, the name of the Lord is spoken of in the same terms as He, Himself.

"I will extol You, my God, O King," exalts Psalm 145, "And I will bless Your name forever and ever. . . . / I will praise Your name forever and ever. / Great is the LORD, and greatly to be praised; / And His greatness is unsearchable" (vv. 1–3). See also Psalms 20:1; 113:1–3; 115:1.

Faith in the name of Jesus activates in us His passion and death. Faith wires us up to the finished work at the Cross, and what Jesus did *for* us is done *to* us. We become what He did. His travail brought spiritual sons to birth, that spiritual "shift" or dynamic transference of believers into the position of Christ. "God . . . made us alive with Christ. . . .

> Faith in the name of Jesus activates in us His passion and death.

And God raised us up with Christ and seated us with him in the heavenly realms" (Eph. 2:4–6 NIV). We are clothed with His holiness "The Lord is my righteousness" (Yahweh-Tsidkenu).

Praying in That Name

We shall now look at faith in the name of Jesus for prayer. But we must understand that this has wide implications. We are commanded, "Whatever you do in word or deed, do all in the name of the Lord Jesus, giving thanks to God the Father through Him" (Col. 3:17). Christianity isn't all prayer and Bible. It means kindness, labors of love, and ranking our neighbors as next to God in our concern. It will be for these practical acts of goodness that the very nations will be judged, as Jesus said in Matthew 25, whereas some who boasted of their works and miracles of faith will be banished from His presence or be nothing.

Nevertheless, we are at present in pursuit of faith, and we are coming to Scripture, for "faith comes by hearing, and hearing by the word of God" (Rom. 10:17). **The Bible isn't written for people of great faith, but for people who have no faith,** and it is here to create and build us up in this vital way.

Jesus taught His disciples to pray (Matt. 6:6–15; Luke 11:1–4). In so doing, He gave us what we call the "Lord's Prayer." One thing is notably missing. It doesn't start or end

> **The Bible isn't written for people of great faith, but for people who have no faith.**

with "in the name of Jesus." It says, "Our Father, hallowed be thy name." Yet Jesus stresses prayer in His name (John 14:14; 16:23, 24, 26). We are instructed to do everything, "whether in word or deed, . . . in the name of the Lord Jesus" (Col. 3:17 NIV).

From this we have clear notice that saying, "We ask it in the name of Jesus," is not essential. To use those words is a statement about our own heart—we ourselves are in His name and speak from that wonderful position.

We are heaven's "in-crowd"! Mere expressions don't impart any power or effectiveness to our prayers or our ministry. Prayer can be silent. It can be a tear or a sigh. God heard the groanings of Israel in Egypt, even though Israel had forgotten His name. We ask in Jesus, for we are in Him when we believe on His name.

When we minister the Word or lay hands on the sick, we do it for Christ because we are doing what He would do. But we take a more dynamic step. We do it not only on His behalf but with Him, clothed with Him, one with Him. That is what "in Jesus' name" means.

Being *in* God was unknown until Christ came. The Old Testament saints, men like Abraham, Joseph, and Job, never remotely spoke of being *in* God. That was an intimacy Israel never dared mention.

> **We are heaven's "in-crowd"!**

The Lord was the lofty One that inhabited eternity, before whom one trembled. The righteous ran to Him and were safe, but this was merely a figure of speech. There was no doctrine behind it of a man's life being hid with Christ in God.

And no one prayed, "We ask it in Thy name" or "In Thy name let this be!" But the way people did pray in the Old Testament is rightly depicted by the book of Daniel:

> Then I set my face toward the Lord God to make request by prayer and supplications, with fasting, sackcloth, and ashes. And I prayed to the LORD my God, and made confession, and said, "O Lord, great and awesome God, who keeps His covenant and mercy with those who love Him, and with those who keep His commandments, we have sinned and committed iniquity, we have done wickedly and rebelled, even by departing from Your precepts and Your judgments." (9:3–5)

Further, the exact prayer is both inspiring and enlightening:

> And now, O Lord our God, who brought Your people out of the land of Egypt with a mighty hand, and made Yourself a name, as it is this day—we have sinned, we have done wickedly! O Lord, according to all Your righteousness, I pray, let Your anger and Your fury be turned away from Your city Jerusalem, Your holy mountain; because for our sins, and for the iniquities of our fathers, Jerusalem and Your people have become a reproach to all who are around us. Now therefore, our God, hear the prayer of Your servant, and his supplications, and for the Lord's sake cause Your face to shine on Your sanctuary, which is desolate. O my God, incline Your ear

and hear; open Your eyes and see our desolations, and the city which is called by Your name; for we do not present our supplications before You because of our righteous deeds, but because of Your great mercies. O Lord, hear! O Lord, forgive! O Lord, listen and act! Do not delay for Your own sake, my God, for Your city and Your people are called by Your name. (vv. 15–19)

Daniel did not pray *in* the name of the Lord. He only prayed *for* His name. His standing before God was that of a righteous man in his own right because of his faith, not the righteousness of the Redeemer. He was heard mercifully with grace as a "man greatly beloved" (Dan. 10:11).

In Acts 10:4, a messenger from God said to a Roman soldier, Cornelius, "Your prayers and your alms have come up for a memorial before God." When Cornelius heard the gospel, the Holy Spirit was poured out upon him and those with him. They were immediately lifted into a totally different relationship, baptized in the very Spirit of God. He was in them and they in Him. That was a dynamic position, not a mere figure of speech.

Old Testament people pleaded their innocence or goodness; that is, they came to God in their own name, resting upon their own virtues as grounds to be heard. For example, Psalm 17:1–3 says, "Hear, O LORD, my righteous plea; . . . / Give ear to my prayer— it does not rise from deceitful lips. . . . / Though you probe my heart and examine me at night, / though you test me, you will find nothing; / I

Christ taught us to pray in a new way.

have resolved that my mouth will not sin" (NIV). And Psalm 26:1, 6 says, "Vindicate me, O LORD, for I have led a blameless life; . . . / I wash my hands in innocence, and go about your altar, O LORD" (NIV).

Christ taught us to pray in a new way. Obviously, the disciples had prayed before, but when they heard Jesus pray, it was like nothing they had ever known. They asked Him to teach them to pray—to show them His way. They knew something was different. Christ prayed, and because of who He was He was heard. So He showed them that because of who He was, they could be heard also—in His name, not like David or Daniel in their own names. It was a new and living way.

When you consider all the history, the greatness, and the work of Christ, and you appreciate what His name represents, then you can see why prayer in His name gives you tremendous backing. Christ Jesus represented us in the judgment and bore desolation. He championed us, though we were a disgrace: "While we were still sinners, Christ died for us" (Rom. 5:8). "The just for the unjust" (1 Peter 3:18). Each comes as one of those for whom this tremendous work was done.

There is power in the name of Jesus, in the way we have explained, when we are in Christ. Repeating it over and over is no different from repeating any other mere word. One word no more moves the hand of God than another, sacred or profane. We might be wise when ministering to

> **There is power in the name of Jesus.**

say, "in the name of Jesus," but it is for those standing by to show the glory is the Lord's alone. Peter healed the cripple and said, "Why do you stare at us as if by our own power or godliness we had made this man walk? . . . It is Jesus' name and the faith that comes through him that has given this complete healing to him" (Acts 3:12, 16 NIV).

In other words, we can come to God in Christ's name, but no name or word can coerce God or force Him to oblige us. That is shamanism and magic to bring about supernatural powers and spirits. God cannot be controlled.

Prayer in Jesus' name is always meant to make the will of God possible. Christ taught us to pray, "Your will be done / On earth as it is in heaven" (Matt. 6:10). There are no miracle formulas to manipulate the Spirit of God or control events. We *must pray,* make intercession and supplications, and seek the face of God in humility and dependence, not pronounce a name like a wizard's wand.

There were healings done when the name of Jesus was never mentioned. Peter's shadow brought miracles. He raised Dorcas from the dead without naming Jesus, but he had prayed beforehand (Acts 9:40). Our expectations are based on what Christ did. Faith brings us into relationship with Him as He works. Faith is the humble handmaid of those who do His will.

chapter 14

Faith and Fear

Fear is natural and good. Like eating and drinking, it is part of our makeup, and it is essential to human life. But just as some people have a compulsion to eat and some have an addiction for drink, some are possessed with fears. To be a glutton or a drinker means that we are guilty, and we are just as guilty when we allow fears to dominate our lives.

Fear Not: Believe Only

We can be hooked on fear. What then? Only faith can get us off the hook. It is the only known antidote to the cobra's bite of obsessive alarm. Jesus said, "Fear not: believe only" (Luke 8:50 KJV). Why "only"? Because that is all we can do—we can only believe when that curse threatens us. It is also all we need to do. It might be a case of great fear, little faith, which leaves us in fearful danger. Fear and worry are killers.

Some fear is good, and some is bad. We get that from the Bible. The book of Proverbs speaks of it as a virtue fourteen times. "The fear of the LORD is a fountain of life," and so on (Prov. 14:27; see also Prov. 22:4; Ps. 111:10). Yet 1 John 4:18 says, "Fear hath torment. He that feareth is not made perfect in love" (KJV).

If you read chapter 20 of the book of Exodus, you will find both aspects.

> Now all the people witnessed the thunderings, the lightning flashes, the sound of the trumpet, and the mountain smoking; and when the people saw it, they trembled and stood afar off. Then they said to Moses, "You speak with us, and we will hear; but let not God speak with us, lest we die." And Moses said to the people, "Do not fear; for God has come to test you, and that His fear may be before you, so that you may not sin." (vv. 18–20)

How can fear be both good and bad? The answer depends on what or whom we fear. To fear God is a wholesome attitude. When you fear the devil, it is a sign that you don't fear God—and there's no faith. The essence of fear is to be faced by something greater than ourselves, some greater person or being or intelligence or power. Whatever it is that we see as the greatest thing is where our fear lies. If we see God as the greatest, we shall fear God more than the devil or men. If we fear the devil most, then we think of him as being greater than God.

Some fear is good, and some is bad.

The fear of the Lord is good. The Lord is great—great in significance, great in wisdom, great in power. To fear God has a salutary effect upon our lives. It is a healthy fear, producing good. We shall not put a foot wrong when we walk before the Lord. If we know He holds us in His hands, we shall "hate evil," as Proverbs 8:13 says. Fearing God makes us godly.

We have a healthy respect for God because of His overwhelming power, but also because of His immovable will. Nothing changes His purposes. He is great enough to crush us but great enough to show us mercy. The fear of the Lord is the only good fear. Other fears—worry, anxiety, dread, and panic—are bad and cause us to live in mortal dread. That is a terrible state of mind, but there is an answer: to fear God and trust Him.

Sin and Unbelief

Sin in Scripture is tied to unbelief. When there is no faith in God, there is no fear of God. Unless we fear God, we shall certainly be sinful. If God is treated with impudence, His judgments and holiness will be mocked. Unbelief in God means no restraint on evil. The cause of any major rise in crime is the loss of belief in the judgment of God. That is the ultimate sanction. Abraham went to Gerar and said, "There is surely no fear of God in this place" (Gen. 20:11 NIV). So he was afraid they would kill him to take his wife.

If we scorn God's power and greatness, we deprive ourselves. God has shown us what He is, not just so we will say, "Aren't You wonderful, God!" It isn't to impress us, but to bless us. This is what He is *toward* us. Unbelief cuts the power off. Paul said he prayed constantly for the Ephesians so that this would not happen: "I pray . . . that the eyes of your heart may be enlightened in order that you may know . . . his incomparably great power for us who believe" (Eph. 1:18–19 NIV).

No one adds anything to his or her life by unbelief. It is a dead negative. Faith particularly acts against the fears that populate the future. A thousand other fears haunt us. We either fear God or we fear everything.

Without faith, people turn everywhere for assurance, even in the most useless and pathetic directions. People turn to the quiet stars, studying the signs of the zodiac, looking for signs of good luck. Isaiah observed all this nearly three thousand years ago and said, "When men tell you to consult mediums and spiritists, who whisper and mutter, should not a people inquire of their God? Why consult the dead on behalf of the living?" (Isa. 8:19 NIV).

> No one adds anything to his or her life by unbelief.

Whom Do We Fear?

The man who fears God fears nothing else. This is what the Bible means in the book of Jeremiah: "Do not learn the way of the Gentiles; / Do not be dismayed at the signs of heaven, / For the Gentiles are dismayed at them" (10:2). We recognize God in all His awesome greatness and His power to save us, and nothing has greater power.

The apostle Paul went to the areas of Europe where there were no Christian believers and preached the gospel. It was an open attack upon the vast, entrenched culture of paganism. The emperor himself was the chief guardian of all the gods. Yet, the apostle of Christ challenged the whole ancient world and disapproved of the might of and impressive array of a cruel world empire.

This unknown Christian, a lone Jew, found Europe and Asia full of fear—fear of spirits and omens, fear of their vengeful and moody gods, fear of the heavens above them, fear of the depths beneath them, fear of the future, and fear of the mysterious

> Without faith, people turn everywhere for assurance, even in the most useless and pathetic directions.

world around them. Paul's fear of God, though, placed him on higher ground, and he said, "For to me, to live is Christ, and to die is gain" (Phil. 1:21). These are the triumphs of faith!

Writing to Rome, the capital that exercised the iron hand of world domination, he said: "I am persuaded that neither death nor life, nor angels nor principalities nor powers, nor things present nor things to come, nor height nor depth, nor any other created thing, shall be able to separate us from the love of God which is in Christ Jesus our Lord" (Rom. 8:38–39).

The New Testament has only one word for fear, and that is *phobeo*. Jesus said, "Don't have phobia, have faith." Jesus had no room for cowards. He said, "Do not be afraid of them. . . . Do not be afraid of those who kill the body but cannot kill the soul. Rather, be afraid of the One who can destroy both soul and body in hell" (Matt. 10:26, 28 NIV).

Once or twice another word for fear is used, the Greek word *deilos,* which means "timidity" or even "cowardice." Jesus said, "O you of little faith, why are you so timid?" We read in 2 Timothy 1:7, **"God did not give us a spirit of timidity, but a spirit of power, of love and of self-discipline"** (NIV).

The Bible's greatest illustration of fearful unbelief and fearless faith lasted forty years. It was like watching a forty-act drama on the stage, depicting the total bankruptcy of faith. We still see them in our mind's eye—those camping tribes of Israel that had escaped the tyranny of Pharaoh. Many a time their wanderings took them close to the border of the promised land. It wasn't that they didn't believe they could go over. They knew it was their right, for God had given the land to them. They were thoroughly convinced. Their faith thus far was almost perfect. But their faith had a fatal flaw—the worm of fear was

> "God did not give us a spirit of timidity, but a spirit of power, of love and of self-discipline."

at the heart of it. Their faith was useless while they feared. So most of them never got there. They panicked. They murmured about their lot but hadn't enough faith to change it. They whined when they could have dined.

When Jesus said, "Fear not: believe only" (Luke 8:50 KJV), it was a profound analysis of this emotion. Normally we say, "Don't be afraid; be brave, have courage!" Jesus didn't just say, "Don't be afraid." He knew very well that fear is part of man's makeup. He said, "Fear not: believe only." During periods of melancholy when, as Scripture says, "neither stars nor moon appear," trust in God is the anchor of the soul. "What time I am afraid, I will trust in thee" (Ps. 56:3 KJV). That is the time to trust.

Fearful Overcomers

Unfortunately, some even by nature are nervous, prone to depression and even panic. There are famous examples such as Tchaikovsky; Thomas Carlyle, the eminent author; and William Cowper, the poet and author of the famous Olney Hymns. Even the prince of preachers, Charles Spurgeon, knew the grip of depression and would make his students laugh because otherwise he said he would weep.

The writer of Psalm 42 may have been afflicted in the same way, but faith also came to his aid. He said:

> As the deer pants for the water brooks,
> So pants my soul for You, O God.
> My souls thirsts for God, for the living God.
> When shall I come and appear before God?
> My tears have been my food day and night,
> While they continually say to me,
> "Where is your God?"
>
> When I remember these things,
> I pour out my soul within me.
> For I used to go with the multitude;
> I went with them to the house of God,
> With the voice of joy and praise,
> With a multitude that kept a pilgrim feast.
>
> Why are you cast down, O my soul?
> And why are you disquieted within me?
> **Hope in God, for I shall yet praise Him**
> For the help of His countenance. (vv. 1–5)

This illustrates a major lesson—faith is not feeling.

When danger comes, fear is inevitable. When our body chemistry sets up a sense of impending disaster, or when we suffer heavy blows and our circumstances are oppressive and dark, or when pain and illness sit with us at the fireside, fear and alarm come as a natural cause and effect. What then does **faith** do? It **takes the shackles from our ankles,** and we challenge their paralyzing grip and go ahead anyway. With God fear will not stop us. Instead, we overcome.

> "Hope in God, for I shall yet praise Him."

A Seven Day Faith

If we are believers nothing can alter that, no matter what hammers and bruises us. Jesus said His followers were to give their lives for Him but "not a hair of your head shall be lost" (Luke 21:18). You—the real you—believes God. The sea's surface is ruffled, but the depths are still. Faith operates without emotional reactions. It secretly imparts strength of mind and peace of spirit. You don't go under, but over. Faith gets us off the hook of fear.

> Faith takes the shackles from our ankles.

Faith isn't just for Sunday, it is for life. Faith is not just for transplanting mountains (Matt. 21:21). It is for *living*. God gives us grace to live, if we believe. The just shall live by faith. Faith is the plus of life and erases unbelief from our hearts and our very being.

Unbelief and atheism never produced an atom of good in the world but **have filled history with misery and horror.** They bring no cheer but damage the human psyche, destroy hope, and lead multitudes to excesses such as drugs and alcohol for comfort and to forget. The inspiration of wonder, mystery, and beauty turns sour with cynicism. The effectiveness of unbelievers in building a better world and in bettering the miseries of the deprived have proved negligible compared to the work of Christians.

Such claim that the West rests on Christian principles, not on Greek ideals. To attack the basic Christian conceptions militates against national stability. It is a betrayal. Such people will fall into the pit, which they have dug. Godlessness filters down from the intelligentsia to the less adequate, and is interpreted in excess and crime. The sanctions of faith in God are the shield and buckler of society.

> Unbelief and atheism have filled history with misery and horror.

What Jesus Christ said and did never prompted one deed of wickedness. Evil men have denied Him and in His name worked horrors, for which Christ will judge them on the Day of Judgment. If there's no God, why work for the future when it will all end in nothing forever? As English philosopher Bertrand Russell admitted after ninety years, the atheist can only build on a foundation of despair. Faith in God has been the highest inspiration, beyond that of love and romance, for every kind of great work known on earth.

That Christ, the Son of God, did not resist the murderous men at the Cross and that He rose from the dead, is teaching so incredible that no one would preach it at all unless it were true. It would never have risen in the first place as a religious faith unless it had all happened. In the ordinary way, such teaching would never have been considered to have a chance in a mocking world. No one would have invented it or thought it would have a chance of ever taking off. The story of a Jew presented by Jews—all despised people—conquered the world because it was true.

Some think that people in Bible days could believe anything because they were so ignorant. They could believe in the virgin birth, for example, because they didn't know what we know. In fact, that is nonsense. They had as much reason to doubt it as we have, and some did. They knew just as well as you and I that virgins can't produce babies. But if God decides to become man, what can stop Him from willing it that way? Is He God or not? Unbelief is not modern. We only have modern excuses.

Likewise, no one can say that miracles can't happen. It calls for total understanding not only of nature and of divine things, but of all mysteries and all history. A Scottish philosopher said he didn't believe miracles happen, because they don't! Logic? How did he know such a sweeping fact? Did he know every remote corner and person on earth and everything that had ever happened, to judge what was a miracle and what was not? The science of one hundred years ago said miracles were impossible. But they also said much else was impossible, and they were wrong. In their minds, television was impossible.

In a broadcast in October 1996, Alastair Cooke pointed out that Einstein himself said that nuclear fission could never be a source of power! We pluck voices, music, and pictures out of the air from across the oceans or a billion miles out in space. Utterly fantastic and ridiculous? They didn't know enough to say so. Skepticism is the conceit of the know-it-all.

Science has not disproved God or the Bible. Scientists as a group are more likely to be believers than any other professional workers. The people who say they can't believe because of science usually know nothing about science! They are still in the nineteenth century and have inherited the opinions of early attempts at understanding the world, settling for opinions now long outdated as if they were infallible. Having a closed mind about the power of God is like having a closed parachute—you jump to a hasty and tragic conclusion.

The old anti-God museums of the Stalinist era in Russia seemed so convincing to atheists. They made Christians laugh, because they were so naive. At Speakers Corner, Hyde Park, London, an atheist challenged God. He said, "I challenge God to strike me dead in one minute from now." He held his watch for sixty seconds. "There you are! There's no God." An elderly lady piped up. "Excuse me— are you married, have you a family? Have you a son?" Yes was his answer to all three questions. "If your son challenged you to fight and kill him, would you do so?" No, he wouldn't. "Then do you think God would want to kill you?"

> To use faith is to be led by the Holy Spirit.

Trust Is Knowing

The way to know God exists is to trust Him. Simply begin believing God, act on it, and doubts will disappear. Live as though there were a God, and you will know there is. Faith in God is our own natural ability made operative by the Holy

Spirit. **To use faith is to be led by the Holy Spirit.** God is not my faith in God, but He comes to me when I am prepared to trust Him. A baby gets strength to walk by walking. We get faith by believing. It isn't something you have, but what you do.

It is a principle explained in a typical paradox of Jesus: "Whoever has, to him more will be given; and whoever does not have, even what he seems to have will be taken from him" (Luke 8:18). If you come in a sullen mood, hoping faith won't work to show the world it won't, well, it won't work.

God will oblige you by not doing anything, if that's your secret wish. You'll get your miserable and mean reward. If you feel sorry for yourself and say God isn't fair to you and doesn't do anything for you, that is how it will be. What you have, you will lose. The last glimmer will flicker out.

Anton Chekhov said, "Man is what he believes." So if people say they believe in nothing, it would mean they are nothing! If we believe in nothing, we live for nothing and get nowhere. But everyone believes something. A man is what he believes. Our believing is shown by what we do.

If Chekhov is right, then we are something if we believe in something. Believing in sport makes us sports fans. Believing in money may make us very much something in the present world system, but nothing to God. Believing in Christ makes us the greatest thing we can ever be—sons of the living God, begotten of Him. By faith we bring ourselves under the estimation of God, who sees us as the purchases of the blood of Christ. We cost Him dearly, but we are dear to Him.

Positive Humility

That, in fact, is the Christian's psychological outlook. A

believer feels he is someone. He is humble but doesn't crawl. He has an eternal destiny. No believer thinks of himself as a breath, a vapor that vanishes at sunrise, as the writers of Psalms suggested. They wrote before Christ came. He "brought life and immortality to light through the gospel" (2 Tim. 1:10). Nothing could give our confidence a greater boost than to believe and know who we are in Christ, i.e., chosen, called, invested with His Spirit, sharing the labors of the blessed Spirit Himself.

At the same time, nothing could keep us more humble than to know that our sins deserved eternal death, but Jesus died for us. We were chosen who were unworthy. Money, brains, and breeding can give us an ego, but the believer knows he is a personality. He is great but without any cause to boast. God has "lifted up the humble" (Luke 1:52 NIV), as Mary sang at the birth of her son Jesus.

True personality arises only in Christ. By accident of birth we may be rich, intelligent, assertive, successful, poor, simple, inferior, or unknowns. That is a temporary state. We can lose it. Rudyard Kipling is the name half the world knows as a matchless writer, but in old age he had to ask what his own name was. What we are by nature is not what counts. **What we are in Christ is the truth about us.** Believing means that each of us, however lowly in station, is given the main chance.

> What we are in Christ is the truth about us.

Some of the greatest people of God were nothing in this world. Billy Bray, simple to the point of eccentricity, a Cornish laborer, is famous a hundred years after his death around the world and regarded as one of the aristocrats of the kingdom of God.

The gospel revival in Latin America is finding men in squalor at the bottom of their social order and lifting them up to positions of influence and high citizenship. Muddled by alcoholism and ignorance, beset by marriage complications, a man comes and sees some old drinking pal now transformed, ministering to a congregation of thousands. He recognizes his worth, redeemed and purchased by the blood of Christ. He believes, is converted, and stands up to be counted.

Millions of such characters cast off their groveling existence as nobodies and become something in themselves, personalities of character and value. Onesimus was a runaway Greek slave trying to lose his identity in Rome but destined for punishment by death. Paul—or rather God—found him. He was elevated, "no longer as a slave, but . . . as a dear brother" (Philem. 16 NIV). We are what we believe. James 2:5 says it all: "Has God not chosen the poor of this world to be rich in faith and heirs of the kingdom which He promised to those who love Him?"

Us and God

What we are depends on who we think God is. Christians know God is like Jesus Christ. When we believe in Him it affects us and makes us like Him, subject, of course, to the limits of human weakness and inconsistency. Something in us strives to reach that standard. **But whatever our moral attainment, we know we stand in high regard before the only One who matters,** our God and Savior Jesus Christ.

Believing in Christ brings out the highest and best in us. It pushes self into the background. Believe in anything else— money, sports, knowledge, humanism—and somehow self always arrives in the foreground. Believing even in a religion can be entirely for the benefit of our own soul, as with the holy men of the East. When we see God as Christ showed Him to us, self-concern begins to die. Our number one interest will not be "number one."

> But whatever our moral attainment, we know we stand in high regard before the only One who matters.

Wisdom, all the qualities that make for the good life, is described between the covers of one book, the Bible. Yet, the keynote is, "Trust in the Lord."

Others did great things, too, but purely as a credit to themselves. God honored those whose efforts sprang from faith in Him. Each of them would never have done what they did, unless they had depended on God. They rose above themselves. What they were was what faith in God made them. It was not what they would or even could naturally do. The greatest miracles of faith are not scientific impossibilities but personal.

It wasn't great faith that lifted them above the average. They were ordinary, everyday folk with ordinary faith—faith that struggled with nail-biting doubt and sweating fears, but which put them into action. They were not saints sitting on cloud nine, spending their time in contemplation, but practical people who changed things around them.

If we are to transact business with God, faith is the coinage we would use. Everyone has a supply of that currency. The Talents Parable (Matt. 25:14–30) is about investing faith. Jesus describes servants with talents given them by their master: one with five, one with two, and another with one. The master went away, and on his return the five-talent man had doubled his capital, and so had the two-talent man. But the other man had only kept and buried his talent and done nothing with it. The employer gave the first two servants a multiplied reward, but he took the talent from the one man and gave it to the ten-talent man.

The focus of the parable is on the man who buried his talent. Jesus is not talking about the ability to play the piano or being good with needlework. He is talking about faith and the man who lost his faith. He "kept the faith," and that is all he did, and in the end he lost it altogether. Faith invested gains interest and increases. People with big faith didn't wake up one morning and find it in their stocking like a gift from Father Christmas.

They used what they had, and it gathered strength and weight. That is always the principle. Moses' first miracle was only to turn his rod into a snake. He took many steps of faith before he led a whole nation into the wilderness, trusting God to feed them.

Jesus and the Littlefaiths

Look at the disciples. In Matthew 8:26, Jesus said to them, "You of little faith, why are you so afraid?" (NIV). This translates a word that is hard to put into English. Jesus called them by the name "Littlefaiths."

Then after the Resurrection Jesus "appeared to the eleven as they sat at the table; and He rebuked their unbelief and hardness of heart, because they did not believe those who had seen Him after He had risen" (Mark 16:14).

Incredibly, though, it was those "littlefaiths" who changed the world. Seeing Jesus alive left them stubbornly unbelieving, but they had a faith breakthrough. At one stage they had asked Jesus to help them. Luke 17:5–6 says, "The apostles said to the Lord, 'Increase our faith!'" He replied, "If you have faith as a mustard seed, you can say to this mulberry tree, 'Be pulled up by the roots and be planted in the sea,' and it would obey you."

It seems that Jesus was correcting their ideas about faith. A mustard seed is a mere dot. Jesus is saying that if we have faith at all, if the dot is there, that's enough! If we have faith at all, it distinguishes us, if only a little. Size doesn't come into it. What increases is not the strength or scale of our faith, but its scope. **Faith is measured by what it covers.** If you have a good electric flashlight, you can narrow its beam and focus it on perhaps just the keyhole of a door, but it can be enlarged and throw light across the whole doorway. Faith at first has a small and limited range, but as confidence comes, it covers a larger area and believes for more and bigger things.

People may have faith for a healing, but have they faith in God for every part and all their lives? Have they faith in God when they are not healed? Perhaps the triumph of faith for some individuals would not be to deliver people from wheelchairs but to be delivered themselves from egotism or bad temper.

> Faith is measured by what it covers.

The apostle Paul was a man of envious trust in God. He healed the sick, cast out demons, raised the dead, and laid hands on people to be filled with the Spirit. He preached in the power and demonstration of the Holy Spirit. We read all that, but most of what he says is about the effects of faith in himself—in other words, what faith had done for his soul.

In 2 Corinthians 12, Paul "boasted" about his experiences and his apostleship. He talked about "the things that mark an apostle—signs, wonders and miracles" (12:12 NIV), but only because the Corinthians put such value on them.

The real signs of his apostleship were what God had enabled him to be. He said, "By the grace of God I am what I am" (1 Cor. 15:10). He had gone to God for healing and it had been refused, but by faith he lived unhealed and displayed the character of Christ in all his career, by faith. He said, "The life which I now live in the flesh I live by faith in the Son of God, who loved me and gave Himself for me" (Gal. 2:20).

It is not the size of your faith but the size of the God you believe in that determines the size of the results. Too many have too small a God.

It would be tedious even to list the gods and the horrors their followers committed to please them. Christians were roasted alive on gridirons to please the Roman deities. Distorted ideas of Jesus Christ Himself, who is the essence of all love, inspired many a murder—the Crusades, the Inquisition, and pogroms against the Jews to name but a few. What these wicked people believed is not remotely connected with the New Testament or the Christ of Calvary. They blasphemed Christ's cross, using it as a symbol of violent purposes—the opposite of what it meant.

We all believe, and belief is a potent force. The God of Matthew, Mark, Luke, John, and Paul is the God revealed in Jesus Christ who laid down His life for us all and retook it, rising from the grave.

> It is not the size of your faith but the size of the God you believe in that determines the size of the results.

What this means to us is life itself, and anyone can attain it. All we have to do is believe in Him and act on it. Your character will change, and so will your likes and dislikes, as evidenced by the following facts about Christians:

- Anybody with faith in the Jesus of the Gospels can never commit atrocities, even against enemies.

- Anybody who loves the biblical Christ is not a nobody, though the world recognizes only the worldly.

- Faith in Jesus is the one pure power that can make the least person great and reduce emperors to nobodies.

- Faith is not just a nice thing, like a box of gourmet chocolate candy. It is the power element of all life and the greatest force for social good known to mankind.

- The most dangerous thing for anybody and any nation is to believe in the wrong thing.

- A door of service fit for a king opens to every Christian believer.

- Ordinary faith is the means by which ordinary people become extraordinary.

- Great faith is only great things done by simple faith. I believe in believing. I believe in believing God.

chapter 15

Faith and the Devil

The devil, supreme commander of the forces of darkness, has numerous fiery darts, against which the Christian has one all-purpose superior counterweapon: faith in God.

Isaiah describes this important weapon. "'No weapon formed against you shall prosper, / And every tongue which rises against you in judgment / You shall condemn. / This is the heritage of the servants of the LORD, / And their righteousness is from Me,' / Says the LORD" (Isa. 54:17).

The question concerning the devil is, What is he really after? What does he hope to gain by evil? Possibly nothing much now and not for very long! He is evil, the opposite of God who is good, and he just does what he does. Once we know the underlying facts about satanic activity, we know how faith will apply.

Satan always had one motive only—domination. God did not make him a devil. He created him a splendid being (Ezek. 28:12–15). Satan made himself the devil. Originally, he rose up, wanting the honors of God (Isa. 14:12–15). He tried to establish his own throne and seduce all creatures in heaven and earth to bow the knee to him. Many in heaven did so. They became his cohorts, his hosts of dark angels.

God's Answer to Satan

God's solution to Satan was strange. He established the physical earth and created men and women. What fragile creatures they were, mere flesh and blood. They looked like an easy target—easily overcome, easily deceived, and easily dominated. That is what they also proved to be— quickly seduced and under Satan's heel. They multiplied, and he captivated them in their ignorance, enslaving them at the beginning of the race. Soon the earth was filled with violence.

But God was by no means outthought. Before such events ever took place, His eternal scheme was prepared. It was so fantastic that the twisted thinking of the devil could never have suspected it. These defenseless short-lived creatures, men and women, were God's master plan. They were to be the instruments of satanic destruction. The Bible focuses on this and explains that,

> God has chosen the foolish things of the world to put to shame the wise, and God has chosen the weak things of the world to put to shame the things which are mighty; and the base things of the world and the things which are despised God has chosen, and the things which are not, to bring to nothing the things that are, that no flesh should glory in His presence. (1 Cor. 1:27–29)

The means would be the very fragility of human flesh. "The Lamb [was] slain from the foundation of the world" (Rev. 13:8). The Son of Man came, bleeding when wounded, as any man bleeds, and bearing even a human name, the name of Jesus. By His gentle submission, "led as a lamb to the slaughter" (Isa. 53:7), the decisive battle was won. An everlasting victory was gained. The scars He bears forever are the pledge and assurance of salvation to a world no longer without hope.

Satan had counted that every knee would bow to him and confess him as Lord. It seemed so easy on this planet, employing weapons of crushing might and war. Instead, came this Man, Jesus, so easily mutilated and taken to death in the flesh. Yet, He proved all-conquering in spirit; let hell do its worst. Today not at the name of Satan, but at the name of Jesus a thousand million bow. Soon every knee and every tongue shall confess Him Lord. Satan is doomed.

Satanic Opposition in Africa

In the West African country of Gabon we faced severe and organized opposition by the local sorcerers and witches. Our meetings were in the evenings, but one afternoon these servants of the devil came to our crusade sites in droves. They stripped naked and danced in frenzy, pleading with the evil spirits to stop our crusade and make it rain. The amazing thing is that the devil couldn't make it rain even though it was the rainy season! One of those mornings I woke up at 5:00 A.M., went to the window, and pulled back the curtain. I wiped my eyes. There they were again, these witches, walking around my hotel totally naked, trying to cast a spell on me. I opened the window and said, "I feel sorry for you. You worked the whole night so hard, and I slept so well!" Isaiah 54:17 says, "'No weapon forged against you will prevail, and you will refute every tongue that accuses you. This is the heritage of the servants of the LORD, and this is their vindication from me,' declares the LORD" (NIV).

Flooding the World with Evil

Meanwhile, the vast ambition of Satan has flooded the world with a multitude of evils. The evil spirit let loose in the world works out in human lives until Christ delivers them. Ephesians 2:2 says, "You followed the ways of this world and of the ruler of the kingdom of the air, the spirit who is now at work in those who are disobedient" (NIV).

The aims of **the enemy** continue, simply because he can't help himself. He is full of cunning. He **gratifies his desires by the domination of human lives.** He injects his spirit, the curse of sin into the world, like the poison of a serpent. From this source come the intractable problems with which politicians, statesmen, social experts, and the rest of us struggle.

He has many strategies of battle. Among them is the occult, which is direct physical manifestation. It includes witchcraft, casting spells, pronouncing curses, possession, various supernatural manifestations, visions, apparitions, fortune-telling, impersonating the dead, and other phenomena of the séance.

The Tricks of the Devil

When Satan resorts to playing physical tricks (which are never of any use), using his human agents, he is used himself.

The devil has to fall into human hands to assert his magic. His dignity has to go along with the cruel practices

> The enemy gratifies his desires by the domination of human lives.

and wild antics of the spirit of men.

I have been in many areas where the occult is part of the culture. Witch doctors using charms have had official license alongside modern doctors. Even football matches in modern African states are reported as the scene of arguments about spells cast on goalposts. As with the ancient gods of pagan times, the spirits are never trusted as benevolent. To ward off marauding spirits engages a considerable industry of superstitions, fetishes, charms, amulets, and the rest. They bring no one peace or assurance.

We have proven constantly that the gospel missiles are "mighty in God for pulling down strongholds" (2 Cor. 10:4). There's a theory that demons are disembodied spirits seeking to inhabit human bodies. Right or wrong, this is speculation outside of Scripture and therefore does not concern us in this book. Scripture seems rather to indicate that only creatures on earth have physical bodies. In some countries, there are those who seek supernatural powers and want powerful spirits to enter and possess them. They put themselves through extraordinary physical ordeals but don't often succeed. It is not so easy to be possessed. God has not made people as vulnerable as that, frail as we are.

Christians and Demons

This is contrary to what many are teaching today. Christians are being told they carry demons with them. Every conceivable ailment and weakness has been named as demon manifestation. It is no great Christian message of joy to be told one is infested with devils! There are those who come weekly for exorcism, as if they picked up demons like bacteria and needed to be disinfected regularly.

Yet, it is true that **the devil** is like a roaring lion. He **brings down any weak runner in the herd** and makes a meal of such people. Opportunity tempts the tempter. If he can resist anything, it certainly is not temptation. Devil possession is a wickedness in which the powers of darkness find perverted satisfaction.

Once occultism grips a nation it destroys all rationality. It can begin with silly fascinations with the Ouija board, or bending spoons and forks. What use is that in our world of weeping multitudes? In the West, one hears of

> **The devil brings down any weak runner in the herd.**

hauntings, poltergeists, knockings on walls, "messages" from the dead, and so on. I think these trivialities and antics must be appointed to the less intelligent denizens of Satan's underworld. But they are initiatory dangers, opening the mind to the fascination of evil forces.

Against all these sordid dangers, **the Christian carries the shield of faith.** It is bulletproof. We enjoy immunity from devil control and enjoy salvation's victory and freedom. We can be bold, impregnable through faith in the redemptive blood of Christ. I pursue the battle right to the enemy's camp. Demonic forces hold sway over thousands, but I challenge the dark hosts of hell

> **The Christian carries the shield of faith.**

with the cross of Christ. Of course, this makes me a target for curses and spells.

Trampling the Lion

I live in the faith of God's covenant as in Psalm 91, which states, "He who dwells in the shelter of the Most High will rest in the shadow of the Almighty. . . . If you make the Most High your dwelling—even the LORD . . . no disaster will come near your tent. . . . You will trample the great lion and the serpent" (vv. 1, 9–10, 13 NIV). The serpent is the devil (Gen. 3:1, 14; Rev. 12:9; 20:2).

Diverting the Truth

However, Satan has a strategy. Occult manifestations are an excellent device to divert Christians from their real job of world evangelism. The occult is a fringe evil in the world, and there are far greater wrongs than this one, to which the answer is the preaching of the Word of God. The occult is not even the cause of world problems. Greed, the love of money, is "the root of all evil" (1 Tim. 6:10 KJV).

The devil sees what the Church is doing. It awoke a century ago to evangelize the whole world. Naturally, we are likely to see satanic opposition of

> Secularism and rationalism are producing the inevitable rise of crime and social upheaval. The devil certainly has come, knowing his time is short.

every possible kind. We have suffered the world's two great wars, and foul anti-Christian movements have arisen such as communism and fascism. World economic fears have distressed every nation. And now, **secularism and rationalism are producing the inevitable rise of crime and social upheaval. The devil certainly has come, knowing his time is short** (Rev. 12:12).

There are vast issues confronting everyone. **He who believes shall not only be saved but bring salvation to the despairing world.** But in many areas, supernatural manifestations of the devil take place to distract Christians.

Satan puts on a fireworks display from hell, and some workers in the harvest stop to stare and others go hunting for demons. It is a sideshow, and we can't afford to make these distractions the center of our work. We are here to make sure everyone we can reach knows the gospel. Jesus cast out the spirits with His word, and that is all the time it should take.

Paul said that we are not ignorant of his devices (2 Cor. 2:11). He and Silas in Philippi refused for days to be drawn into direct conflict with a demon spirit. Finally, they thought it best to cast the spirit of divination out of the possessed girl. As a result, their successful evangelism in the city was cut short, and they had to leave.

> He who believes shall not only be saved but bring salvation to the despairing world.

In our own campaign services, spirits manifest themselves. It is the same trick, to distract attention from the preaching of the gospel. We don't stop preaching to carry out a few exorcisms. I am a harvester for God and don't stop the combine harvester to catch a mouse. When victims begin to divert attention from the Word being preached, they are removed from the gathering. Personal workers deal with these people away from the crowd, expelling the spirits.

Exorcism is our duty, but it is only one element in preaching the gospel to every creature. Neither exorcism nor healing is the whole gospel. We follow the example of Jesus in such things. His earthly mission was the kingdom of God. He established His purpose with a direct onslaught on the works of the devil, never seen until that time. **He called us to be fishers of men, not demon hunters.** There are Christians who seem more demon-conscious than Jesus-conscious. They talk far more about what devils do than what God does. Exorcism has a subtle danger, infecting some people with pride, who just talk of the spirits fleeing at their com-

> He called us to be fishers of men, not demon hunters.

mand. Jesus warned us in Luke 10:20 to rejoice not that the spirits are subject unto you, but rather rejoice because your names are written in heaven.

Tricks of the Enemy

We could not name all the devices of wickedness. They occupy the entire world press every day. Having done all, we stand in faith. When the world falls to pieces, the Christian survives. The victory is our faith. We have Paul's vivid picture of the Christian church's armor, in the book of Ephesians, chapter 6:

> Finally, my brethren, be strong in the Lord and in the
> power of His might. Put on the whole armor of God,

that you may be able to stand against the wiles of the devil. For we do not wrestle against flesh and blood, but against principalities, against powers, against the rulers of the darkness of this age, against spiritual hosts of wickedness in the heavenly places. Therefore take up the whole armor of God, that you may be able to withstand in the evil day, and having done all, to stand. Stand therefore, having girded your waist with truth, having put on the breastplate of righteousness, and having shod your feet with the preparation of the gospel of peace; above all, taking the shield of faith with which you will be able to quench all the fiery darts of the wicked one. And take the helmet of salvation, and the sword of the Spirit, which is the word of God. (vv. 10–17)

Obviously, if faith can shield us from Satan's arrows, then he will want to knock the shield out of our hand. If he can't do it completely, he will try to trick us into dropping our faith guard for a moment or to shatter the shield and leave us with only scraps and tatters of faith. Without faith, we are open to deadly personal damage—morally, psychologically, and spiritually.

The Bible as Our Weapon

Jesus quoted the Bible in His direct encounter with the devil in the wilderness. That is our example, but not without faith. The Pharisees and scribes knew Scripture well enough in their way, but Jesus said they neither knew the Scriptures nor the power of God (Matt. 22:29). The reason was, as we read in Hebrews 4:2, that the word "was of no value to them, because those who heard did not combine it with faith" (NIV).

Unless faith in God comes with the Word, we can throw the whole Book at the devil, and he'll only laugh. "This is the victory that has overcome the world—our faith" (1 John 5:4). It also quenches the burning arrows of the enemy.

A life poised on the living God emboldens us, firms the shape of our character, tightens our resolve, and gives us the daring to live above the mundane. Faith in God is a spring of crystal cleansing goodness flushing the gutters of society and disinfecting the sinks of human foulness and wickedness. Men of faith have a higher value effect than men of business or of genius.

> Unless faith in God comes with the Word, we can throw the whole Book at the devil, and he'll only laugh.

Men of faith are the real warriors against this world's wrongs. **One convert today can prevent a war tomorrow.** Suppose Adolf Hitler or Joseph Stalin had been won for Christ as teenagers! Faith represents trouble for the lords of wickedness. Imagine a scene in the counsel chambers of hell with the prince of darkness putting drive into his princes and powers saying, "We must find an answer to the number one problem, faith. It is the super weapon against us. We must spike it and sabotage it at all costs. This kingdom can never make headway against the kingdom of God so long as the simplest person goes on trusting in God."

> One convert today can prevent a war tomorrow.

Well, the powers of darkness concoct many a scheme to overthrow or bypass our "Maginot Line" of faith.

Fighting the Fight

The Bible tells us to "Fight the good fight of faith." What is that? First Timothy 6:9–12 shows us. It is to flee from the love of money by which some have wandered from the faith with foolish and harmful desires, and to pursue righteousness, godliness, faith, love, endurance, and gentleness, and to take hold of eternal life.

Many of our struggles come from the world and the flesh as well as the devil. Recurring temptations perhaps arise with the pressures of the world and even our own nature as we tempt ourselves. James 1:14 proves this by saying that each one is tempted when, by his own evil desires, he is dragged away and enticed. As for the devil, James 4:7 later says to resist the devil and he will flee from you. How do we resist the devil? James went on to tell us, admonishing us to "cleanse your hands, you sinners; and purify your hearts, you double-minded. Lament and mourn and weep!" (James 4:8–9).

The same method is described in 1 Peter 5. We are told to be "not greedy for money, but eager to serve . . . submissive . . . [clothed] with humility . . . self-controlled and alert. Your enemy the devil prowls around like a roaring lion looking for someone to devour. Resist him, standing firm in the faith . . . and the God of all grace . . . will . . . make you strong, firm and steadfast" (vv. 2, 5, 8–10 NIV).

> Many of our struggles come from the world and the flesh as well as the devil.

This is where the battle is—in us. We overcome the devil by guarding ourselves with the shield of faith, throwing our trust upon God, and thus giving the devil no place in our lives. What is the use of expelling demons if we are full of pride in doing so?

Should we fail and sin, blaming an indwelling demon will not do. When Paul deals with personal failures, he never mentions the devil or exorcism. He says we are to put our sinful habits into reverse: "Let him who stole steal no longer" (Eph. 4:28); keep the Ten Commandments, give generously, pay revenue taxes, and "put aside the deeds of darkness . . . behave decently . . . not in orgies and drunkenness, not in sexual immorality and debauchery, not in dissension and jealousy. Rather, clothe yourselves with the Lord Jesus Christ, and do not think about how to gratify the desires of the sinful nature" (Rom. 13:12–14 NIV).

> Sin has one remedy, and that is to "repent and believe."

When pastors deal with moral failure by exorcism instead of by discipline and rebuke, they are far away from the New Testament, for "The soul who sins shall die" (Ezek. 18:20)—no excuses, and no blame laid on a demon.

Sin has one remedy, and that is to "repent and believe." There is one answer to the work of the devil, "They overcame him by the blood of the Lamb and by the word of their testimony" (Rev. 12:11).

The Faith Fact

chapter 16

The Faith Fuse

Faith is like a wiring system that carries power into our lives. The wiring carries power but does not create it. Faith is similar. It only carries power. **Faith in itself is not power, but it links us to the power source.** There's no link to God's power without faith.

The Power Source

The source of power is God in heaven. On the first recorded New Testament campaign, Philip the evangelist came up against Simon, who used sorcery (Acts 8:9–10). Simon was astounded at the miracles of Philip in the name of Jesus, professed salvation, and was baptized and went along with Philip.

Then Peter and John came to Samaria, laid hands on converts, who received the Holy Spirit in such a powerful demonstration that Simon could witness their experience. He coveted the ability to lay hands on people for

> Faith in itself is not power, but it links us to the power source.

the Spirit himself and offered the apostles money. Peter rebuked Simon for thinking the gift of God could be purchased with money. Since then, "simony" has been the name for the purchase of church office.

But there is more than that to the story. Simon wanted power, whether by sorcery or money. His desire is universal, and people resort to many means for it. The general aim of the New Age groups is to tap into sources of power—mind power, cosmic power, earth force, occult power—by a thousand theories and practices. Some Christian believers also seek the power of God by dubious processes.

Power and Prayer

Some think that power is generated by religious exercises, such as prayer, fasting, or separation. The idea is that the longer they pray and fast or the more they avoid "the things of the world," the more power they will experience.

For example, power is expected in direct proportion to time spent in prayer—two hours brings twice as much power as one hour. It is a process of generating power by exertion; the greater the labor, the greater the current—power in commercial proportion to hours spent. How much does God pay per hour? Power is thereby a credit to Christians; the display demonstrates the labor. The more the power, the more admirable the person—a cause and effect basis.

The teaching of Jesus is nothing like that. He said we must not suppose that we will be heard for our "much speaking" and that we can't calculate the effectiveness by how much we say or how long we talk to God. Of course, we are creatures of time and must spend time in prayer. On some occasions, it may be many hours before we feel satisfied, but prayer measured by the clock, for the sake of praying a long time, is a work of the flesh, not of faith. **Without faith a month of prayer is not as good as five minutes with faith.** No amount of time can make up for lack of faith. It is a matter of faith, not time.

Some wait in silent meditation to draw strength. This is not praying but mysticism, "waiting" for any impression that floats into one's awareness—a voice, revelation, vision, or to absorb spiritual vibrations, etc. This openness carries no guarantees that what comes is from God.

It is not the Bible way. Revelation independent of Scripture is the way of the false prophet. People claim God has spoken to them in their mind. He can, and does, but not just at our beck and call. This claim of mystical and subjective guidance and knowledge has worked havoc all the way through history and was the worry of apostles all the way through the New Testament. It is the way Islam and Mormonism and Buddhism and other religions came. The claim to spiritual power has to be tested by the Word of God.

> Without faith a month of prayer is not as good as five minutes with faith.

Power is also sought from holy places or objects. People visit shrines and look at the relics of saints or try some physical link with men of God. Yet, these long-dead people never even believed their bones could cure people or planned that they should.

The holiness of saints did not impregnate their clothes or other objects for people to benefit from, and their relics don't ooze grace or give the living a leg up the stairs to heaven.

First- and Secondhand Power

"Pilgrimages of grace" are notably absent from the New Testament. The Christians of old never believed that any such powers could be transmitted from them. It would only be secondhand power, a kind of castoff from the dead. Why not desire firsthand power? If we do what the apostles did, we shall get what the apostles got. Peter said that God had given to the household of Cornelius the same gift as the apostles had on the Day of Pentecost (Acts 11:17). "The promise is to you and to your children, and to all who are afar off, as many as the Lord our God will call" (Acts 2:39).

> The Holy Spirit does not infect us, and we don't receive it by contagion.

Blessing does not brush off on us from physical contact. **The Holy Spirit does not infect us, and we don't receive it by contagion.** He comes to us Himself and dwells in us. The Spirit comes when sought directly from God by faith in the name of Jesus.

Triumphant Divine Power

The mystic realms are not where disciples find power—it is available on earth. The Spirit of God makes our *bodies* His temples; He doesn't float around in some superconscious area of our personality.

Christ's atoning death and triumphant resurrection made available to us all the divine power and aid we could ever need. For two thousand years, Jesus has proven to be all that He said He was and has done all He said He would do. If we come to Him and ask, not sit hope- fully in some ancient

> Christ's atoning death and triumphant resurrection made available to us all the divine power and aid we could ever need.

stone building trying to absorb the vibes or seek association with a third party living or dead, He will fulfill His promise and endue us with power. In fact, Scripture does not encour- age placid religious inactivity of that kind at all. He sends us out to do His work, and that is when power and strength and everything we need are given.

Power comes with truth, which dawns with the Word of God. There is no power without the Word. If our cup is to overflow, we need a cup, and the Word is that vessel. It isn't a loose or dispersed energy

> Power comes with truth, which dawns with the Word of God.

collected by soaking in a quiet and deep meditation.

The mystics talk about the "cloud of unknowing" and the "dark night of the soul." But Jesus said we should know and not walk in darkness. Ordinary people on this plane of mortal existence know Jesus. Their simple faith touches Christ, not some mysterious level of airy spirituality. If we go to Him, He meets us on our human level as flesh-and-blood creatures, not as mere spirits. And He does not cast us out.

Take Peter, for example. Peter had a revelation—which is a form of power. How? What? It was more than a spiritual illumination about nothing in particular. It was about Jesus. And he didn't sit like Buddha to find out. It was there, and he perceived who He was. The Holy Spirit takes the things of Christ and reveals them to us. They are positive and include the assurance of salvation, the sense of Christ's presence, the whisper of the Holy Spirit in our deepest heart, the gifts of the word of knowledge, wisdom, and prophecy. These are the defined responses of God to our faith.

God does not play a game of hide and seek. Christ said, "I am the way, the truth, and the life. No man comes to the Father except through Me" (John 14:6), and that "he who believes in the Son has everlasting life" (John 3:36). He is not the Great Unknown, but the God who sent Jesus and who wants us to know Him.

> God does not play a game of hide and seek.

We need His strength, His enabling, His energizing—and for this He reveals Himself. Jesus is not a strange voice echoing from the beyond. If we call upon Him, He answers us and *does things.* He saves, guides, and heals. We throw ourselves upon His promises, and His arms are already there, open to welcome us.

Power Seekers

The pride of man is to possess powers independent of Christ and to be as gods. For instance, earth-power seekers believe they are part of the god Gaia, the planet Earth, and profess to absorb the earth energies. The basic sin of mankind is to stand alongside God with our own light and power, our own glory, and feel we are self-sufficient.

God, Himself, is the source of power and is found only by faith in Christ. **Jesus is both our Guide and the Way.** He is the "one Mediator between God and men" (1 Tim. 2:5). For that office, He paid the infinite price. He knows the way because He trod it. Christ explored every inch of it from heaven to earth and from earth down to hell. We cannot ignore Him. To beat out our own path to the well of the Water of Life is neither necessary nor successful. The all-sufficient Christ opens it to us and says, "Only believe."

God Is the Open Gate

That is the wonderful Christian truth because the door to God is no longer closed. We no longer have to strive, searching the dimensions of heaven, waiting and hoping. Ring the bell of God's gate and the front door is immediately opened. God says, "Welcome!" He is not hard of hearing or hard to find. He has made known His name and His address.

The world has strived to create its own spirituality and gather strength from its own sources. But any higher quality of life can only be found at the source, with the God who made us.

Doing Things God's Way

God has set up His own way. The purpose of Christ was to make war against the devil and destroy the evils that cut us off from the life forces of God. This mighty work was

> Jesus is both our Guide and the Way.

accomplished at the Cross. His final cry was, "It is finished!" (John 19:30). The Greek word for finished (*tetelestai*) does not mean "ended." It means it is completed or perfected. The edifice was ready and the last cornerstone put on.

He descended into death to confront death and defeat it. Then, victorious, He rose from that experience and ascended for us. And to where? To the right hand of power. He was seen alive as the evidence of His victorious battle on the cross. Within days of His ascension, the blessings of heaven poured upon men and women and transformed them. Faith in the victorious Christ changed the disciples from cringing and hunted creatures to bold proclaimers of the gospel, dauntless warriors of the truth.

Their faith was in the promise of Christ. They obediently waited for the empowerment. They had no idea what it was or how it would come, but they sat with open hearts, certain Christ would not let them down—obedient faith. That faith became power lines, carrying the surge of divine glory into their souls. The Day of Pentecost was the switch-on day of the "power stations" of Christ's work on earth.

The book of Acts chapter 10, exemplifies the conductivity of faith. An officer in the Roman occupying forces called Cornelius was a God-fearer, that is, a foreigner who went along with the Jewish religion—as much a convert as Gentiles were allowed to be. He had many virtues: giving liberally to charity, praying, fearing God, and being righteous, devout, a fine influence, and respected by all.

In the list of his attributes, one thing is conspicuously absent—faith. Like his rabbi teachers, he would think that salvation was an achievement. A life of prayers and charity would add up to divine favor at last. Religion was a mere liturgy.

Then, a messenger direct from heaven entered his house. The bold soldier was terrified, but the angel said, "Your prayers and your alms have come up for a memorial before God" (Acts 10:4). God knew, and it had all been entered to his credit in the divine audit.

However, Cornelius needed far more, and God had far more for him. The messenger simply said, "Send for Peter"— and Peter had the keys to the kingdom of God. Peter came. He used the keys; that is, he preached the good news of Christ. Cornelius had gathered everyone around. Now, for Peter this episode was a series of revelations. Peter said, "In truth I perceive that

> He descended into death to confront death and defeat it.

. . . in every nation whoever fears Him and works righteousness is accepted by Him" (Acts 10:34–35). But accepted for what? Divine appreciation only? This is the real question.

Cornelius told Peter that they had all come "to hear all the things commanded you by God" (v. 33). What Peter said was just that—the words God wanted Cornelius to hear. He gave Cornelius and the people with him an account of Christ's work, ministry, death, and resurrection, which is still the church's message to the nations. Peter had put the key in the lock, and then he turned it by saying, "All the prophets witness that, through His name, whoever believes in Him will receive remission of sins" (v. 43).

Belief Opens the Door

Peter's audience had believed every word, but as soon as he mentioned "believing," the door of the kingdom opened. "The Holy Spirit came on all who heard the message" . . .

and those who came with Peter "heard them speaking in tongues and praising God" (vv. 44, 46 NIV). Cornelius found the vital thing. It is not what we give to God, but what He gives to us. The faith contact was made, the circuit was completed, and the power of the Spirit flowed through immediately.

On one particular occasion Jesus was talking to religious men who thought their studies would bring them the reward of eternal life. They hoped to work their way into the kingdom, handling the synagogue's scrolls of the Scriptures. In their hands daily, they held more than six thousand promises of God, and yet they were no better off for any of them. Then Jesus said,

> "I do not receive honor from men."

> You search the Scriptures, for in them you think you have eternal life; and these are they which testify of Me. But you are not willing to come to Me that you may have life. **I do not receive honor from men.** But I know you, that you do not have the love of God in you. I have come in My Father's name, and you do not receive Me; if another comes in his own name, him you will receive. How can you believe, who receive honor from one another, and do not seek the honor that comes from the only God? Do not think that I shall accuse you to the Father; there is one who accuses you—Moses, in whom you trust. For if you believed Moses, you would believe Me; for he wrote about Me. But if you do not believe his writings, how will you believe My words? (John 5:39–47)

It is a familiar old story. People set up their own little generators and switch them on to do the work of Christ.

Meanwhile, the mighty turbines of heaven could meet every need of power in their lives.

We can now look at a few "good works" named in Scripture and learn in depth the secrets of belief and action:

- **Prayer** (James 1:6–7 NIV): "When he asks, he must believe and not doubt, because he who doubts . . . should not think he will receive anything from the Lord." Jesus said, "When ye pray, believe" (Mark 11:24 KJV).

- **Hearing the word of God** (Heb. 4:2): "The word which they heard did not profit them, not being mixed with faith in those who heard it."

- **Seeking God** (Heb. 11:6): "He who comes to God must believe."

- **Worship** (Heb. 11:6): *Worship* in Scripture is not merely something done in church once a week. The word itself means to serve God. To worship God in a place of worship is part of that service, but all service must be an act of faith, for "without faith it is impossible to please [God]."

- **Keeping the commandments** (John 6:29): "This is the work of God, that you believe in Him whom He sent."

- **Tithing** (Luke 18:9–14): Jesus described two men. One was a tax gatherer, knowing he was sinful, praying for mercy. The other was a religious Pharisee who claimed God's attention because he gave tithes. The Pharisee prayed about himself, "I . . . give a tenth of all I get." Jesus judged the situation. "I tell you that this man [the tax collector], rather than the other [the Pharisee], went home justified before God" (NIV). We can give tithes in unbelief, as did the Pharisees.

Operating in Faith

Believing goes on in the heart and mind, unseen, until it actuates something we do. The power of God operates when we operate by faith. The famous chapter of Hebrews 11 was written to show that the ancients of faith not only believed, but also dared.

In Luke 17:5 the apostles said to the Lord, "Increase our faith." Christians have been wanting this kind of faith in bulk ever since. So what does Jesus say? "If you have faith as a mustard seed, you can say to this mulberry tree, 'Be pulled up by the roots and be planted in the sea,' and it would obey you" (Luke 17:6).

That must have puzzled the apostles. They wanted big faith, but He spoke of the smallest thing they knew. By the way, He did not refer to the mustard seed because it was very small. The issue was the contrast between massive faith and small (but living) seed. He wanted to hammer home that faith is never a matter of size, bulk, or weight. What shape is a thought? Believing is what you do, not a substance. Perhaps the apostles wanted faith to tackle bigger tasks. But it doesn't come beforehand. Scripture speaks of the proportion of faith (Rom. 12:6)—it is proportionate to the job at hand, index-linked to the need. Like running and needing more air, your intake increases automatically.

> Active faith needs impossibilities.

Size loses its meaning even for the task when it is a faith-task. The bigness of a hill, a house, and a molehill are all one to a bird flying over them. By faith we "shall mount up with wings like eagles" (Isa. 40:31), and nothing is insurmountable. **Active faith needs impossibilities.** Religious faith, faith just in church, doesn't have enough impossibilities. Robust faith grows in the outside weather, or it will be a sickly plant.

Conductivity, Not Size

Perhaps you have never seen a mustard seed. You may need your glasses to see one. But the people to whom Jesus spoke knew seeds. It was an agricultural world. Jesus spoke their farming language. But today we are a "high-tech" society, and our expressions are scientific. Jesus spoke the language of the people, and today our expressions come from technology. No doubt today Jesus would use our common speech.

Jesus spoke two thousand years ago about the "mustard seed," a small thing with mighty potency. Maybe today He would talk about a microchip or fuse to illustrate His teaching. "If you have faith as small as an electric fuse you could transplant trees from soil to sea." Like the mustard seed, the value of a fuse is not in breadth or length. The key is "conductivity." **Faith transfers the power of God to wherever it is needed.**

> Faith transfers the power of God to wherever it is needed.

A fuse is made of a metal, such as silver wire, which offers low resistance to current. Low resistance means high conductivity. Translated into the spiritual, the lower our resistance to the Word of God, the higher the power rating.

The higher our resistance in obedience to the Word, the lower the operational power of God.

Low Word Resistance

A fuse with high resistance would either carry no power at all or else soon blow. When we resist the Word by unbelief, the power of God can't come through. If we say we believe in the Word but disobey it, we negate our faith. It blows the fuse. The power of God is little when the Word of God means little to us.

Whatever else may be true, one thing is absolutely beyond contradiction: **Christianity is a power religion or it is nothing.** Liberals, teachers of rationalist doctrine, rely on logic. The apostles relied on the power of God. "The world by wisdom knew not God, it pleased God by the foolishness of preaching to save them that believe" (1 Cor. 1:21 KJV).

> Christianity is a power religion or it is nothing.

The Faith Fuse and Doubt

Our head can be our doubt box. Reasoning is too uncertain an instrument for vital personal relationships, especially with God. It is like using a shovel, instead of a telescope, to read the night sky. When people turn to science with its algebraic equations, geology, or philosophic deductions to approve religious faith, it is ridiculous. What can these things possibly have to do with spiritual experience? **Science has no equipment to handle relationships with God.** You may as well use a corkscrew to study music.

How do we believe or not believe in anybody? By mathematics? Have you ever felt you can't trust somebody but you can't put your finger on why? It is a gut feeling under your skin. A higher self, intuition, is at work and triggers off an alarm. Thomas Brown penned, "I do not love thee, Doctor Fell. / The reason why I cannot tell; / But this alone I know full well, / I do not love thee, Doctor Fell." But we believe in somebody else for the same reason, but what that is, we may not know.

> Science has no equipment to handle relationships with God.

Instinct never warns us against Jesus. When we "get wise" to Him we want to come closer. Knowing Him better, we heart-warm to Him. "We love Him because He first loved us" (1 John 4:19). What unbelievers say means no more than what the barometer says. The proper way, the only possible way, is to trust Him. **The effective center of true life is the heart, not the brain.** "With the heart one believes" (Rom. 10:10).

Faith by Hearing

Faith isn't just "believing" with nothing special in mind. It is believing *unto* something and *for* something. The Word of God gives point, direction, and purpose. To borrow the words of Longfellow, without the Bible, faith is like an arrow shot into the air that "fell to earth, I knew not where." In fact, the Bible is the only Book that gives faith a positive goal. One wonders what some religions propose to do for folk who believe. They become a religious treadmill, believing for the sake of believing.

The apostle Paul was aboard a sinking ship, but he

said, "I have faith in God" (Acts 27:25 NIV). It wasn't a kind of defiant sentiment. It was specific—all on board would be saved. "We must run aground on some island" (Acts 27:26 NIV). It was rather different from the man on an Atlantic crossing in a storm, who asked the captain if they were safe, and the captain, trying to reassure him, said, "Sir, we are in the hands of God." The man replied, "Is it as bad as that?"

> The effective center of true life is the heart, not the brain.

Maxims of Faith

Here are some basics:

- To be believers, we should know what we believe and whom we believe.

- The most basic lesson is that we must take the Word of God at its face value.

- Without knowing God's will, faith is impossible.

- The Word is the eternal will of God.

- To question Scripture is to question the only guide we have and to question God.

- The Word of God is an ultimatum, not an object of discussion.

- Bible truth is not decided by democratic vote or consensus. It is "settled in heaven" forever (Ps. 119:89).

- The Bible is the constitution of the kingdom of God, and no two-thirds majority of any parliament on earth can change it.

Resting on Authority

The Bible makes no bones about it and insists a thousand times on its own divine authority. The prophets who spoke, for example, were not offering their private political opinions, but "men spoke from God as they were carried along by the Holy Spirit" (2 Peter 1:21 NIV). They used the phrase, "Thus says the Lord." The Jewish conception was of a God of awful holiness, and they trembled before His awesome greatness.

Unless they had an overwhelming sense that God had sent them, no prophet of Israel would dare to claim to be the mouthpiece of this almighty Being. Only absolute certainty would open their mouths. Jeremiah declared, "I said, 'I will not make mention of Him, / Nor speak anymore in His name,' / But His word was in my heart like a burning fire / Shut up in my bones; / I was weary of holding it back, / And I could not" (Jer. 20:9).

The Authority of Christ

God spoke and heaven and earth materialized. "He spoke, and it was done; / He commanded, and it stood fast" (Ps.

33:9). Then John's Gospel makes the tremendous assertion that "the Word became flesh" (John 1:14). The same voice that created all things now spoke to us. What He said comes with absolute authority. It is the Word of the Lord.

When Christ spoke, He said heaven and earth would pass away but not His words (Matt. 24:35). He was not like the prophets. They spoke *for* the Lord, but Christ spoke *as* the Lord. The prophets said, "Thus saith the Lord," but Christ said, "Truly, truly I say to you." The Jews listened to Moses, but Jesus went beyond Moses, "Moses [said but] I say" (Matt. 19:8–9).

There was something else different. The prophets were sent with a message, but Jesus *was* the message. The prophets spoke about the Lord, but Jesus spoke about Himself. He not only brought the Word of God, but He was the Word of God. He didn't point to the way; He was the Way. Jesus was not one of the roads that led to God. He was where the road led.

> God spoke and heaven and earth materialized.

That is why we have no right to doubt the Word of God or bend God's exclamation mark into a question mark. If we do so, "To whom shall we go? You have the words of eternal life" (John 6:68), as the apostle Peter recognized. **We either obey or die.** Using our technology language, we blow the fuse and suffer a lifelong power failure. The heating fails, the lights go out, communications cease, the systems break down, and cold, eternal night settles in.

> We either obey or die.

Liberal teachers scorn people of faith. They say we have an "authoritarian religion." But do they teach without any authority? All learning is based on authority, either divine or human. Some trust in the authority of scholarship, but nothing is less trustworthy. Their arguments are steps in sand. Scholars never agree with one another. The Word of God has been a light to a hundred generations, and that lamp has never flickered.

Wisdom itself loses its way without revelation. For instance, a modern poet, Philip Larkin, tried it. He was an atheist. Journalist Martyn Harris wrote about Larkin just before he died in 1996, saying his godlessness left him "drunk, suicidal, self-obsessed and paralyzed by misery." Larkin himself described his desolation facing a bleak eternity in his poem "Aubade." He waited for "the total emptiness forever. The sure extinction that we travel to, and shall be lost in always."

Faith in God seems a vague sentiment, but it solidifies into reality. We can "cast ourselves upon the ocean of the unknown" with wonderful assurance. Jesus said, "If anyone loves Me, he will keep My word; and My Father will love him" (John 14:23).

> Wisdom itself loses its way without revelation.

Learning and Getting Somewhere

The major lesson I personally had to learn when arriving in Africa from Germany was to unlearn the business of questioning God. We question politicians but believe God.

For example, Christ said in Mark 16:17–18, "These signs will follow those who believe . . . they will lay hands on the sick, and they will recover." It is not for me to consult intellectuals for their approval, but to obey the Word. **I do what God says, and then He does what He said.** God changed the polarity of my heart and spirit and then began to use me to shake whole nations. God used the rod of Moses, and so He uses us when we follow His orders. I see His power at work time after time. My faith fuse has held, and the currents of blessing have flowed through my life to millions of precious people to redeem their souls by the blood of the Lamb.

Why Look on Us?

We can't generate power by anything we do—music, worship, atmosphere. As soon as two or three gather in His name, He is there. Immediately, the throne is built, and we don't need to take an hour of worship to build it or pull power down from heaven. It is impossible for Christians even to meet in His name without Christ being there in power.

> I do what God says, and then He does what He said.

If it were our work to produce the power of God, we would be the power generators. But Christ gave us power. We are not called to go into the entire world with our own little power plant, so folk will think how wonderful we are.

We can parade our own charisma and make the sparks fly for an hour, but soon our power plant will run out of fuel and begin coughing and dying. **We are not generators, but conductors.** "Of His fullness we have all received"; He is "the fullness of Him who fills all in all" (John 1:16, Eph. 1:23). We are channels, not the source. "As the branch cannot bear fruit of itself, unless it abides in the vine, neither can you, unless you abide in Me" (John 15:4).

Power Stations

God does not need any of our energy dynamos. He has His own, two of them, right here on earth: the Cross and the empty tomb. Power flows forever from those sources, day and night, without power cuts or breakdowns. The voltage is unfailing and reliable. There is no fluctuating flow "from the Father of lights, with whom there is no variation" (James 1:17).

Here's our full equipment:

- The spiritual energies of the Cross and the Resurrection
- The power lines of the Word of God
- The fuse of our faith, the vital link

They give us:

- Power for every need
- Power to change lives
- Power to break vicious habits
- Power to heal the sick
- Power to light the storm-darkened highway of life

No power known on earth, created in test tubes or in industry, can do any of those things. **The power of God is the** great force on earth to deal with the intractable problems of living.

At a conference, I overheard some young people say, "We must be switched on for Jesus. All it takes is to be switched on for Him." I turned to them and said, "Yes, it is good to be switched on for Jesus, but it is more important to be plugged in. Switching on for Jesus will be useless unless we are plugged in. We must be connected first." Being switched on to ourselves produces no current.

> We are not generators, but conductors.

The Live Link

The power of God coming through the Word reaches the faith fuse first—and that could be the preacher. That tiny bridge of power can become very warm. A preacher of the Word is the first to feel that warmth. He burns with the charge. He is likely to show it, and he should. He is a communicator not of his own thoughts, but of the power of God. He should be a live wire. A preacher is a man having an experience with God in public. If he represses his exuberance and puts polish, elegance, and propriety first, he should remember these are not fruits of the Spirit, but joy is. "The joy of the LORD is your strength" (Neh. 8:10), not weakness.

If an experienced electrician touches a live wire and gets a shock, he may just say, "Oh!" But anybody having an electric shock for the first time is likely to react in a more dramatic fashion. God's power is not a fiction but a fact. It is the greatest reality we know.

If God does manifest Himself, what would anybody expect? A graveyard? Or resurrection? Dynamic life may seem unseemly at first. But when people experience the flowing current of divine blessing, they will appreciate why. Nobody knows what it is like to meet Jesus Christ until they do. One exuberant preacher was told, "Please restrain yourself!" He replied, "I am restraining myself!"

Completing the Circuit

Great power lines stretch across a whole country carrying perhaps 110,000 volts on a single cable. Day and night the huge power turbines are feeding the vast system, harnessing the forces of coal, water, oil, or nuclear fission, housed in towering buildings. All that! Then, at home a tiny wire fails, and everything in your house stops, without power. The greatness of God, the

> The power of God is the great force on earth to deal with the intractable problems of living.

greatness of the work of Christ, the greatness of the Word of God are all there, but without faith, as small as a fuse wire, none of that greatness avails. The circuit is broken. The power bridge is down.

If the faith fuse fails, the dynamic of God is defused and will be refused by those to whom we preach. Indeed they could be confused! Take the Word, put in the faith fuse, and the power of God comes through—there be light, warmth, energy, salvation, healing, strength, blessing.

Power Anywhere

Not long ago, I went into a very smart hairdressing salon. Two ladies were there, and one of them began to cut my hair. Typical of hairdressers, she talked while working and asked whether I was a businessman. My reply was, "I am a man of God." It was perhaps a good, hard knock, but it broke the ice, and we were launched. In a short time, I was leading both of these ladies to Christ. They knelt in the hair on the floor while they prayed the prayer of salvation. When I left the shop, I heard one with tears in her eyes saying to the other, "That man of God came in for a haircut—what a glorious day!"

I went out very happy and moved. Then I met my colleague Peter van den Berg. I said to him, "Peter, I see you need a haircut, too. Go and get your hair cut in that salon. I've led two women to Christ in there. Go and do the follow up!"

"If you have faith as a mustard seed," Jesus said (Matt. 17:20). So little! Our faith is no towering sensation that everybody sees and gasps. It is the hidden fuse. But by it, the energies of heaven flow into the world. God uses main fuses and sub-fuses, but never subterfuge. Wherever we are, the hidden attitude of our hearts is God's missing link.

When Christ was at the entrance of Lazarus's tomb, Martha, the sister of Lazarus, had doubts and fears that Jesus could do what He was attempting—to raise him from the dead. Jesus said to her, as He continues to say to all of us, in good times and in bad: "Did I not say to you that if you would believe you would see the glory of God?" (John 11:40).

We are at the door of undeniable faith. The opportunity on the other side is immeasurable. Will we step through? We must!

About the Author

In 1972 as a young missionary, Reinhard Bonnke was gripped by a vision of Africa coming to know Christ. During the course of his ministry, he has spoken to nearly thirty million people and has seen nearly six million new converts recorded at these crusades. He has also held personal meetings with thirteen African National Presidents.

DenCo z.com SP. warfare Bees